THE MONEY CULTURE

The
MONEY
CULTURE

MICHAEL LEWIS

W · W · NORTON & COMPANY
New York · London

Printed in the United States of America
First published as a Norton paperback 2010

Excerpt from H. L. Mencken, *Prejudices: Fourth Series*,
reprinted by permission of Enoch Pratt Free Library, Baltimore,
in accordance with the terms of the will of H. L. Mencken.

For information about permission to reporduce selections from this book,
write to Permissions, W. W. Norton & Company, Inc.,
500 Fifth Avenue, New York, NY 10110

For information about special discounts for bulk purchases, please contact
W. W. Norton Special Sales at specialsales@wwnorton.com or 800-233-4830

Composition and manufacturing by
LSC Communications
Book design by Jacques Chazaud
Production manager: Louise Mattarelliano

Library of Congress Cataloging-in-Publication Data

Lewis, Michael (Michael M.).
The money culture / by Michael Lewis.
p. cm.
1. Brokers. 2. Finance. I. Title.
HG4621.L48 1991
332.6'2—dc20   91-13331

ISBN 0-393-03037-7

ISBN 978-0-393-33865-2 (pbk.)

W. W. Norton & Company, Inc.
500 Fifth Avenue, New York, N.Y. 10110
www.wwnorton.com

W. W. Norton & Company Ltd.
15 Carlisle Street, London W1D 3BS

8 9 0

This volume is affectionately dedicated to
the woman who taught me that there is more credit
in making the right enemies than in making the wrong friends:

my mother.

The iconoclast proves enough when he proves by his blasphemy that this or that idol is defectively convincing—that at least *one* visitor to the shrine is left full of doubts. The liberation of the human mind has been best furthered by gay fellows who heaved dead cats into sanctuaries and then went roistering down the highways of the world, proving to all men that doubt, after all, was safe—that the god in the sanctuary was a fraud. One horse-laugh is worth ten thousand syllogisms.

—H. L. Mencken

Contents

―――――――――◆―――――――――

THE MONEY CULTURE

Introduction

At the beginning of the last decade there was a kind of moral fad in parts of the United States that spread almost immediately to the capital cities of industrial Europe. The age old Anglo-European taboo of handling money was shoved offstage by the sheer force of events in the financial world, clearing the way for a new money culture.

The change most obviously affected the behavior of the well-to-do. The fortunate offspring of the ancienne noblesse, who would have been expected to enter the quiet professions or perhaps a genteel family business, went into predatory trade. Heirs to old New England fortunes raised so far from financial reality that they could hardly balance their checkbooks suddenly wanted to stage hostile raids on America's corporations for the greater glory of Goldman Sachs. Of course, it wasn't only the rich who wanted to experiment with financial terrorism. The rich were just the tracer dye in the water, the clearest evidence of cultural drift.

All those young studs with gleams in their eyes who streamed from Harvard and Stanford onto Wall Street are said to have been greedy. I don't believe this for a minute. Greed for money—for the sake of money alone, rather than its attendant status—requires years of practice to learn. It is a rare trait in young people, especially in those who have never tasted deprivation. The money was important, but mainly as a way of keeping score. The appeal of the new financial world to a young person was its promise of drama. For a brief moment there was this corner in the world economy that didn't require you to grow up the way American businessmen usually grow up. You didn't have to be Babbitt. You didn't have to submit to the Establishment.

On the contrary, many of the trendsetters in the new money culture had antiestablishment credentials; that counterculture gurus such as Jerry Rubin drifted in the 1980s onto Wall Street was no accident. Bruce Wasserstein, the patron saint of the hostile takeover, had worked for Ralph Nader. Michael Milken, who created the market for junk bonds, left Wall Street for California, where he built an empire in the spirit of bohemia upon the foolishness of Establishment bankers and captains of industry. He said that finance was an art form—an art form! Lewie Ranieri, who created the market for mortgage bonds, had to be ordered by his chief executive officer to buy himself proper business suits ("I hate these suits," he told me). You had only to spend about five minutes with these people to realize they didn't see themselves as part of orthodox business culture. They saw themselves romantically, as guerillas in the corporate jungle. They were fanatics with attitudes.

Their style of business travelled much better than they did themselves. By 1984 any city with a financial district was swarming with versions of the American idea of success. Paris had its golden boys; London had its yuppies. Young Italians, Germans, Swedes, and Swiss poured into London looking for work in the European branch offices of American investment banks. From Tokyo there was token resistance—the elite graduates of Tokyo University were slow to forego the safety and discomfort of Japanese corporations for the high drama of American investment banks. But they did. And before long a style of capitalism had become one of America's leading cultural exports. It had all begun with seemingly dry and boring changes in technology, financial regulation, and levels of debt in America, but it ended with a revolution in everyday commercial behavior.

The pieces collected in this book are set mainly in and around the new money culture. They all relate, in one way or another, to the marvelous commercial madness of the 1980s. I've ordered them geographically, with a section each on America, Europe, and Japan. I won't pretend they were written with the intention of herding them between hardcovers; but I don't intend to apologize for them either. After all, this is how I make my living these days.

PART I

NEW WORLD

In 1985, the average income of the ten best paid people on Wall Street rose from $29 million to $51 million, and everyone involved traded in his gold American Express card for platinum. One night early that year, Stephen Joseph, a partner of the now bankrupt Drexel Burnham made what seemed to be a routine business trip to Minnesota. The only unusual thing about it was that he visited his client in his home and stayed late for drinks. In the course of the evening Joseph happened to mention how much he expected to be paid. The number made an impression on the client's seven-year-old-son, who was eavesdropping on the staircase. Two days later the boy handed his father an essay he had prepared for school. It was called What I Want to Be When I Grow Up and almost perfectly captured the mood of the day.

> I want to be an investment banker. If you had 10,000 sheres [sic] I sell them for you. I make a lot of money. I will like my job very, very much. I will help people. I will be a millionaire. I will have a big house. It will be fun for me.

While those words were being written, I was interviewing for jobs on Wall Street. I eventually landed at Salomon Brothers, where I occasionally helped people, but more often helped myself. In my spare time I wrote. Several of the pieces included here were written in the evenings, after a day spent in a training program in New York or on a trading floor in London. A daytime job was an enormous and perhaps unfair advantage for a writer. It enabled me to watch people when they didn't know they were being watched and disabused me of any illusions I might have had about Wall Street or its leaders, who were my bosses. In my defense I can only say that my bosses knew what I was doing all along; one even took it upon himself to read my pieces before they appeared in print.

There was one exception. After the stock market crash of October 1987 I surreptitiously published an article entitled "When Bad Things Happen to Rich People." I used a female pseudonym, Diana Bleeker, mainly because I didn't want to be fired. I assumed that the rampant chauvinism of the Salomon Brothers traders would blind them to the possibility that a man might hide behind the name of a woman. I admit that while it was all very cowardly, I thought it was all very clever, as well as pleasing to my mother, since Diane Bleeker was the first two parts of her maiden name. It would have been even more clever and pleasing if I had spelled it correctly and if the article, when it appeared, had not announced beneath the byline "Diana Bleeker is a pseudonym."

Anyway, the piece contained a paragraph or two of criticism of Salomon's Chairman and CEO, John Gutfreund, as well as a few lines of description that could have come only from someone who had seen the Salomon Brothers trading floor. Skepticism about one's bosses, however well-earned, is not universally appreciated, even in the upside-down world of an American investment bank. The day the article appeared it was copied and distributed on our trading floor. Before long I had several calls from traders who wanted to know if Diana Bleeker was me. Then something happened that I never expected. Instead of being angry or upset, John Gutfreund—give the man credit—was amused. He thought Diana Bleeker was *funny*. He thought she was so funny that he rose during a lunchtime meeting of Salomon's 109 managing directors and read aloud from her piece. Apparently they didn't all find her equally amusing.

A couple of days later the managing director responsible for me flew the red eye from New York to London. In itself this wasn't unusual. He'd take the overnight flight every few months to check on us and maybe do a bit of shopping. But normally he'd nap in his hotel room for a couple of hours before he visited the office. This time he came without the benefit of sleep. I recall that he looked as if he were running on amphetamines as he stormed through the office door.

The man was troubled. That made two of us. He came straight to my desk—also unusual as protocol demanded he check in with the head of the office before hobnobbing with us grunts. He smiled his most disarming smile. And he said, "I would just like to know one thing. Did you write that article?"

"Think about it," I said. "Do you really want to know?"

And he thought for a minute. Then he said, "No, don't tell me. Do not tell me. I don't want to know."

Now he'll know.

Christmas
on Wall Street

The first ghost arrived five minutes late. Jeremy Gaunt was doubly irritated. The ghost of Christmas Past was due to arrive at one! Of course Jeremy Gaunt was vaguely aware that Christmas was a time of peace on earth and goodwill toward men and that sort of thing. But it was also bonus time on Wall Street. And Jeremy had just put down the phone to his branch manager at the Chase Manhattan, so he knew that his four hundred fifty thousand dollar bonus hadn't hit his account. Too true! One more day's interest gone, uncompounded. Jeremy Gaunt wasn't all that thrilled with his bonus to start with. After all, he had worked on Wall Street for five whole years—well, four and a half—but when a bonus check didn't arrive on time. . . . You can just imagine the state Jeremy was in when the ghost first spoke.

"We're leaving now," said the Ghost of Christmas Past.

"Hold on, hold on," said Jeremy, "let me get my jacket."

"Where we're going," said the ghost, "you won't need it."

Instantly, they were in a dark room at Tellson's, an old British banking firm. Several elderly gentlemen with bad teeth encircled a pile of gold coins. They conversed on a matter of high finance.

"Mine!"

"No, mine!"

"Gimme!"

"Get away!"

"Gimmee . . . Gimmeegimmeegimmeegimmee!!!"

The discussion continued in this vein for some time. Finally, one of the men—the one furthest from the pile—spoke a full sentence.

"Sirs! What if there is nothing left for our customers?" He was ignored.

"Ghost," Jeremy shouted over the din, "where are the yuppies?"

The ghost pointed to the corner of the room. There sat a young man in a green eyeshade staring at a ledger. "When they took a young man into Tellson's London house," wrote Charles Dickens in *A Tale of Two Cities*, "they hid him somewhere till he was old. They kept him in a dark place, like a cheese, until he had the full Tellson flavor and blue mold upon him."

"Ghost," said Jeremy, "I can't bear this. Can we go someplace nice?"

In a flash Jeremy found himself hovering in the air beside a different sort of ghost altogether. This ghost refused to answer any of Jeremy's queries. Instead he pointed to . . . the rear window of a limousine. Jeremy could hardly believe it—the limo was moving at speed, yet he and the ghost were able to float off its rear bumper as if it stood completely still. And there, before his eyes, was . . . Marcus Drysdale from interest rate swaps! Marcus was stretched out along the back seat.

"You know Morris," he was saying (Morris was the chauffeur), "when I graduated from college I was lost. I figured if I didn't get a Wall Street job, I was looking at twenty-eight grand a year from IBM. It was scary." Morris nodded.

"You know what I just got paid Morris? Do you?"

"No sir."

"C'mon Morris. Take a guess."

"I wouldn't know about that Mr. Drysdale."

"Seven hundred grand Morris. Read my lips: Seven, Oh, Oh."

"Very good sir."

"Damn right it's good. That idiot Gaunt only got four fifty."

At this Jeremy spun on the ghost of Christmas Present. "Can you believe that. I get four fifty, he gets seven. I've been robbed!" The ghost shrugged. There was nothing he could do.

"Goddamit," shrieked Jeremy, "you're supposed to be the

ghost of Christmas Presents. Do something!"

All of a sudden Jeremy was suffocating in the exhaust of the limousine. Or at least that's how it seemed. But when the smoke cleared there was, lo and behold, a third ghost!

Of course, Jeremy realized what had happened. He had been gypped by the ghost of Christmas Presents. This new ghost looked too poor to do anything about Jeremy's reduced circumstances. Four fifty was small change next to Drysdale's seven. Life was so unfair!

"I am the ghost of Christmas future," said the ghost of that name.

"I got out of futures and into cash last week," said Jeremy. The ghost just shook his head and pointed.

Jeremy saw that they must have travelled about forty years. He and the ghost stood in the corner of an office beside a Wall Street trading floor. Unless he was mistaken, that was *him* sitting with a five-year-old girl on his knee. He looked like a preppie Grandpa Walton.

"Ghost," said Jeremy, trembling, "is . . . that . . . me?" The ghost would not respond.

"No," said Jeremy, "it couldn't be. I was going to retire on my capital in 1991. I was going to *do something.*" Still quavering, Jeremy walked outside the office and stared at the name plate on the door. Jeremy Gaunt, it said, and underneath: Vice-Chairman.

"Oh my god," said Jeremy, head in hand. "Oh . . . my . . . god . . . *vice-*chairman?" The ghost stared.

"Ghost," said Jeremy, "tell me, please, what do I have to do to become chairman?" The ghost shook his head.

Jeremy's eyes returned to the scene in the office. Perhaps it wasn't so bad. The little girl was spellbound by her grandfather. Sweet child!

"Poppywoppsy," she asked, "is it true you worked on Wall Street during the Money Wars?"

"Yes my dear, it's true."

"Is it true that there were monsters who ate money for break-fast?"

"Um . . . of course. . . . Yes my dear, it's true."

"Did you know *them?*"

"Well, a few of them."

"Poppywoppsy. What did *you* do?"

"I was a bond salesman."

"Eeeeeeeiiiiii! Put me down!"

"But I never sold *junk* bonds, Lizzie Boo! I never sold junk!" Jeremy was screaming when he woke up. And he looked around and saw that he was lying on his eiderdown quilt, in his three-bedroom co-op, on the Upper West Side. And he knew that he had been dreaming, and it was Christmas day, and his bonus was earning interest, and everything was going to be all right. No way Drysdale had been paid 700 grand. No way.

Leave Home Without It: The Absurdity of the American Express Card

The American Express cardmembers' booklet strives for an erotic tone, sort of like a financial Kamasutra, divided by chapter headings. Some of these—*"Experience the Flexibility of No Pre-set Spending Limits"*—alert the mind to new possibilities. Others—*"Verify and Record Expenses with 'Country Club' Billing"*—confuse but in a flattering way, like having too many people grooming you at once. One especially caught my eye: *"Enjoy the Recognition."* The guide elaborates. "American Express Cardmembers enjoy a prestige that is associated with no other card. Cardmembers may feel this specialness as soon as they begin to use the card. When you use the card you may even notice that often you are served better and are accorded an added degree of respect."

That sounded like what I was after. So I took my green American Express Card to the local liquor store and bought a bottle of champagne. The salesman ran the card through his machine and handed me the charge slip to sign. But he gave me no feeling of specialness. Perhaps he is subtle, I thought. There was only one way to find out. I took another bottle of champagne from the rack but this time handed him my Visa card and braced myself for scorn. Instead, he brightened.

"Oh you have Visa! Do you mind if we tear up the other slip and put both bottles on that?"

So much for recognition. So why else do 32 million people pay $55 and up each year for an American Express card?

Let's be reasonable. There are two simple criteria for judging a charge card. The first is how much it costs. The second is what you can do with it. By any objective measure, American Express is at the back of the pack. Its annual "membership" charges of $55 for a green card compares with between nothing and $20 for a Visa or Mastercard, depending on the issuing bank. (Visa and Mastercard, unlike Amex, are franchisers.) Even a Visa gold card is on average $15 cheaper than the Amex green. For Amex gold you pay $75; for the exalted platinum—"by invitation only"—$300.

Why is Amex pricier than the competition? First, Visa and Mastercard are credit cards; the banks that issue them make their profit mostly by lending money to consumers at exorbitant rates. The cards are primarily a way to attract borrowers. Amex, on the other hand, is a charge card, meaning that you have to clear your account each month. With perverse logic, American Express tries to persuade people that a charge card is somehow superior to a credit card. "Since you settle your account promptly," says their mouth-watering booklet, "you never have to pay any finance charges." But of course you never have to pay any finance charges with your Visa either, if you pay up each month. A bank credit card can be used as a charge card, but it has the nice option of a loan if you want it.

The main reason for the $55 price tag is simply that the Amex card is marketed as a luxury good and has been since its birth in 1958. But in the early years it genuinely *was* a luxury good. Universal charge cards didn't exist. The first (purple) Amex card was meant primarily for use with airlines, hotels, and restaurants around the world. It provided a unique and useful, if rarefied, service, and the 253,000 people who bought one probably were special. Trotting the globe and paying with plastic was, after all, unusual.

Now it is not, as anyone who has seen an airport can testify. What's more, the role of the plastic card has changed as people use it not only for travel but for everything and not only to buy but to borrow. Today there are 220 million major credit cards wedged into American wallets. In the last two years alone the volume of goods charged to cards nearly doubled, from $286 billion to $440 billion. Economies of scale have enabled high-volume, low-cost providers of the service such as Visa and Mastercard to move in. There are 190 million Visa cards in the world and just 32 million Amex. Amex's market share has fallen steadily for the last ten years; most recently it is 19.8 percent, down from 21 percent in 1987 and 22 percent in 1986.

Were American Express selling a normal good, the first thing it would do to meet the competition would be to lower its fees. But the company maintains that it isn't selling a normal good. "The card," as the booklet says, "is much more than a simple payments instrument. . . ." Oh, really? How so? "[I]t is based on a membership principle." In other words, Amex is selling snob appeal, which has a logic all its own. And when you are selling snob appeal, trying to compete on price is not merely futile, it is self-defeating. An American Express card that cost no more than a Visa card would be worth even less.

Another rule for the snobbery seller is always to provide buyers with at least a flimsy justification for paying through the nose: mink is warmer, my new BMW is ten mph faster than my old one, I can read the diamond arms on my wristwatch more easily, and so on. You must create the illusion (and only the illusion, as cheaply as possible) that your product is different. No one actually wants to say, "Yes, I own an American Express card because it makes me feel superior." One wants to say, "I like Amex because of its Country Club billing" (which, by the way, simply means that you get copies of individual receipts each month).

As Visa and Mastercard have spread in recent years, Amex has tacked on all sorts of weird gifts of questionable value to shore up the myth that its card is superior. Unfortunately, bank cards have matched Amex freebie for absurd freebie (though they haven't marketed them with equivalent skill or force, which is why you are probably more aware of the benefits of Amex). The result is reminiscent of the battle among gas stations for business in the 1970s, when they gave away free drinking glasses that small children busted against back seats of family station wagons.

For example, insurance: whether it is automobile or life, the nice thing about insurance is that the cost to the credit card company is fairly trivial, but describing it can fill up pages in a brochure. If you use your green card to buy a plane ticket, you are insured against precious bits of you falling off in transit—$50,000 for a hand or a foot, $100,000 for an eye and a hand or a foot, and so on. Die while using your American Express card and your heirs are in the chips. That is, if it occurs to them to collect. Since most American Express cardholders probably already have life insurance, their Amex policy is superfluous.

Amex's latest, and most heavily hyped, freebie is the so-called "Purchase Protection Plan." Anything bought with an Amex card is insured for 45 days after the purchase. "If you lose your new prescription sunglasses," says the Amex booklet, "or if someone accidentally spills a drink on your new Oriental rug, all is not lost if the purchase is made with the American Express card." The service is a little silly: why would you want to insure against someone spilling a drink on your new Oriental rug only for the first 45 days? But Amex—and also Visa, which has matched it—may be playing with fire here. Purchase protection is like money-back guarantees in that it relies heavily on people not exploiting the system. I called a woman at the Amex plan and told her I had just backed my new Jaguar, paid for with a green card, into a salt water lake. It looked bad. Could she reimburse me? She sounded reluctant. "Well," she said, "I can help you file a claim." The system is too new to evaluate, but it is a safe bet that it will either be generally ignored or canceled.

Another distinction Amex makes much of is "No preset spending limit." No doubt this is genuinely handy for a few high rollers, and it is the single service that the bank cards don't offer. But most people I know (maybe I know the wrong people) can survive happily on the limits of $5,000 and more offered by bank credit cards. This only makes sense. We eventually have to pay for the things we buy (or at least that's the idea), and the limits imposed by bank cards are calculated with a generous eye on our ability to pay. Anyway, just because the limit isn't "pre-set" doesn't mean there isn't a limit. Have you ever actually tried to charge a Jaguar to a green card? Good luck.

The real purpose of a charge card isn't these various extras but simply a convenient way to pay for things. Sadly, a card performs this basic service more often if it doesn't say American Express on it. Visa, for example, is taken by seven million merchants worldwide. A mere 2.6 million take Amex. The reason for the sweeping victory of the bank cards over Amex is that Amex charges shops nearly twice as much for the privilege of accepting their cards. Amex's

1988 average "merchant discount" was 3.29 percent while Visa charged 1.7 percent. What annoys shopkeepers even more is that American Express takes far longer than the banks to pay up—which adds to the merchants' cost and to Amex's profits.

Ask Visa about their merchant charges and you get a straight answer. Ask Amex and you're told, "We don't release that information." (I got the 3.29 percent figure only by threatening to use instead the fee paid by shopkeepers in my neighborhood, which is 5 percent.) And the gap between Visa and Amex has been growing. In 1982 Visa's merchant charge was 2.41 percent and American Express's was 3.4 percent.

Eighty-eight billion dollars' worth of goods and services were charged to Amex cards in 1988, a tribute to the power of marketing. American Express billed merchants, on average, about 1.6 percent more than bank cards would have (not including the free loan implicit in delayed payments). In other words, of the $3 billion or so Amex collected from merchants, about $1.4 billion represents a sort of surcharge that could have been avoided if we all used Visa. This surcharge is passed on to the customers and is shared by all of them, not just those who use the American Express card.

Amex is about to launch a new ad campaign featuring a handful of expensive stores—Bergdorf Goodman, Neiman Marcus, K-Paul's Louisiana Kitchen—that take *only* American Express cards. The campaign is thoroughly disingenuous. The message underlying the ads—that Amex will get you into more places than the competition—is the opposite of the truth. Moreover, the ads don't say *why* these stores only accept American Express. The reason is that in exchange for agreeing not to take Visa or Mastercard, the stores have had their Amex merchant discounts cut to the bone and receive a fortune in free advertising.

In other words, even at the very few stores that only accept American Express, it isn't a matter of Amex making life more convenient for its own members. It's Amex making life *less* convenient for the rest of us. If there is any shop in the world that takes *only* the American Express card without being bribed by American Express, I'd be surprised. Without an especially sweet deal from Amex, there's no reason not to accept bank cards and every reason not to accept American Express. In fact, the only reason merchants do take

American Express is that some customers still insist on paying with it.

I put the cold comparative facts of the matter to an intelligent friend, who is also a senior executive at American Express. I asked him why people should pay $55 for something they could have for $20 or for free. He said, "Intangibles," by which he means the elusive and vaguely erotic Recognition and Specialness: shopping at Bergdorf's, "Country Club" billing, Oriental rugs, and prescription sunglasses. American Express markets its card as a badge that says, *I am a financial success,* like pulling a fat wad of c-notes in a silver money clip from your breast pocket, only not as gross. In a current Amex television commercial, a man and his kid sister are finishing what looks to be a $60 restaurant meal:

> BROTHER: Dad was afraid I'd find a starving artist up here.
> SISTER: Oh, dad was worried?
> BROTHER: Okay, I admit I was a bit worried when my little
>   sister took off on her own.
> SISTER: I'm not so little anymore.
>   *(The bill arrives at the table.)*
> BROTHER: Here . . . let me get that.
> SISTER: No way. It's mine.
>   *(She drops her Amex card onto the tray)*
> BROTHER: American Express huh? . . . I'm going to stop
>   worrying about you.

We are supposed to imagine what brother might have said if sister had paid with Mastercard or Visa: "Visa, huh? . . . you can use that to buy polyester pants suits at K-Mart, can't you?" Or worse: "You peasant. You soil the family name."

As evidence of basic solvency the American Express card is at least plausible. As a mark of distinction it is absurd. The card, says the brochure, is "much more than a simple payment instrument, it is based on a membership principle." Yet this is a club with 32 million members. It's not easy to manufacture "prestige" at such a high volume. It requires that we be told many millions of times that the club includes famous people such as Tip O'Neill, Wilt Chamberlain, and Helen Hayes, in whose reflected glory we may bathe. It requires 100 public relations specialists and (I am told) $350 million a year in ads and promotion. That's about ten dollars a year per card. Cardholders should know that nearly a fifth of their annual membership fee goes into ads to tell others: *you can join our exclusive club.* Sort of defeats the purpose.

American Express caters to a contradiction in terms: a popular craving for an elitist symbol. It isn't a club. It is a corporation with shareholders. It wants more than anything to grow and grow. But by growing it debases its currency. The only way around the conundrum is to stratify the membership. Thus American Express has given us an entire class system. Green spawned gold in 1966, gold spawned black in 1984, and black spawned platinum in 1985. (Visa and Mastercard followed with gold alone.) When platinum arrived there were about 500,000 gold card holders. One day there will be 500,000 platinum card holders (there are about 80,000 at present), and Amex will give us the diamond card. The impulse behind the scramble into a higher class of cardholder is the same as the one behind the purchase of an even bigger diamond collar for one's poodle, except that even a $300 platinum Amex card is status on the relative cheap and therefore relatively mass marketable.

And what about the 80,000 platinum cardholders? What exactly do they get for their $300 a year other than a sharp intake of breath from the lady at the checkout counter? It is not immediately obvious. The Amex literature reads a bit like a clever résumé: a few hazy accomplishments are made to fill up a lot of space. There seem to be five extra benefits accruing to platinum. (1) A $10,000 line of credit, which any rich person could get from a bank in a flash. (2) A "travel counselor who will book honeymoons, arrange personal vacations, and fulfill unusual travel requests," i.e., a travel agent, a service that is free even for poor people. (3) "An itemized record of activity at the end of each year"—well, useful perhaps. (4) "Preferred welcome: priority treatment offering deluxe services and special amenities at a select group of distinguished hotels and restaurants in the U.S., London, and Paris"—a fruit bowl, cheese, and crackers. (5) "Complimentary nonresident membership in 26 exclusive private Centurion clubs." I defer to Groucho Marx.

Thorstein Veblen explained it all years ago: in affluent societies the economic struggle "is substantially a race for reputability on the

basis of . . . invidious comparison." One function of the flashy cards
is to reflect glory and cachet on the cards beneath them, to attract the
hoi polloi, like celebrities at a fund-raiser. The most Veblenesque of
all members in the American Express family of plastic was the so-
called "black privilege card." A handful of these were issued in 1984
to gold card holders who also had some minimum number of millions of dollars in American Express bank accounts. The black card
was, as an Amex executive put it, "ultraexclusive." It enabled holders to "do anything they wanted." For instance? "Well, they might
need a helicopter sent to the middle of the Sahara to pick up their
son on safari. We'd do that." Black card members were also able to
arrange private shopping sprees late at night at expensive stores such
as F. A. O. Schwarz and Neiman Marcus. Classy people who didn't
want to flaunt their wealth found this useful. Small wonder, then,
that Imelda Marcos and Adnan Khashoggi were two of the leading
users.

Eddie the
Chop House Boy

Eddie Braverman is probably the most likable guy ever to haggle over the bill during his mother's funeral. The trouble began when Eddie wanted to pay with a check. The mortician knew about Eddie's checks. Eddie's checks bounced all over Brooklyn, from the Dime Savings Bank to the Orchard Fruit Store. The mortician insisted on cash, then dug in his heels for a fight to the death. But so did Eddie. And in a graveyard on Coney Island Avenue the two men pushed Eddie's check back and forth across the mortal remains of Winnie Braverman while the rabbi and a couple of Eddie's friends watched, mortified. In the end, of course, Eddie had his way. Eddie always had his way. The mortician wasn't about to send the rabbi packing and drag Eddie's mother all the way back to the morgue. *He* had a reputation to consider. The mortician took Eddie's check. It bounced.

Eddie had a stomach for trouble. If he was less concerned than most Wall Street stockbrokers with his reputation, it was partly because his reputation never prevented him from doing business. When I asked Eddie why this was, his wife, Patricia, who was present at the outset of our interview, hit the roof. "Eddie, I don't think we should talk to him until we've discussed compensation," she said. Then to me: "What will you pay for our story?" Funny, people are always having to pay for dealing with Eddie.

"Just calm down, Patricia," said Eddie. "We've got to start somewhere. . . . There'll be movie rights later." Patricia stormed from the room and slammed the door. Eddie leaned back in his swivel chair, which swallowed his elfin frame, and smiled. It was a smile that made you, too, want to smile. It was maybe the most dangerous smile I'd ever seen.

Over the last twenty years Eddie, with that smile, had suckered some of the least likely suckers in the world. He had worked for forty-four different Wall Street firms, by one count. He had defrauded many of the firms, along with scores of small investors. Forty-four firms—that number takes a while to digest. He says he "can walk into any firm in the world, and they know who I am"; and if it isn't true, it's at least amusing. They probably know his lawyer as well.

And they most certainly know a few of his stories. Eddie Braverman stories are all over Wall Street. A few of them, like the one about the way he buried his mother for free, are entirely true. Others, like the time he sent the bloody bull's head in a box to his former boss at E. F. Hutton, are Eddie's inventions. Many are believable, but only because it's hard to imagine why anyone would make them up. Was the mob really after Eddie for drug money? Had an angry fellow broker at Wellshire Securities really dangled Eddie by his ankles from an eleventh-story window? Had Eddie really contracted hepatitis B from a bad needle and infected an entire office at Lehman Brothers? Had Eddie really been fired from Oppenheimer when the boss caught him in the boardroom rubbing belly buttons with a secretary? "Yeah, yeah, that happened," says Eddie, a bit too eagerly. "And there are more."

Eddie may be crazy, but he was hired far too often to be dismissed as an irrelevant crackpot. Wall Street saw something in Eddie that it liked. Several firms hired Eddie twice, and one firm hired him three times, despite the file at the National Association of Securities Dealers (NASD) on him with the size and psychological complexity of a Woody Allen script. Eddie had bounced checks. Eddie had burned customers. Eddie had burned employers. Eddie had forged a drug prescription in 1978 to feed his habit. Eddie was a convicted felon. Eddie was married to a convicted felon (Patricia had been the female half of a team of burglars billed by the *New York Post* in 1978 as Bonnie and Clyde). Then there was the sinister-looking fellow in a trench coat who turned up on Wall Street every

so often looking for Eddie. He'd linger in reception areas and mur-
mur darkly about how he represented a group of men who felt that
Eddie "had to be stopped." He sometimes claimed to be "writing a
book" about Eddie. Right. *How to Swim with Concrete Shoes in Two
Easy Steps.* There was a long list of good reasons not to hire Eddie.
It was ignored. The reason, say the people who ignored it, was simple: "He's one of the best salesmen I've ever seen," says a broker
who worked with him at Citiwide Securities and at Steven Andrew.
"He knew how to give a story regardless of whether it was true or
not."

"Everywhere the guy goes, misery follows," says the man who
hired him at Dean Witter. "But the guy knows how to bring clients
in."

"He's one of the great bullshit artists of all time, and people in
our industry are gullible and stupid," says a man who hired him to
hunt heads for Wertheim Securities. "He's really slick."

"One of the great ganefs of all time," says a broker who worked
with Eddie at Rooney, Pace, and Oppenheimer. "One of the great
frauds of all time. Watching him reminded me of watching Robert
Morse in *How to Succeed in Business Without Really Trying.* He was a
remarkable salesman."

Eddie himself is more modest. He says all it took was a lot of
chutzpah and the right look. When he needed work, he'd simply
appear unannounced in the reception area of some Wall Street sales
office and demand to see the boss. Eddie says that often the boss was
so relieved that he wasn't a federal marshal or an SEC prosecutor
that he would hire him on the spot. "But you have to look right,"
says Eddie. "You have to have the uniform. You can't be casual. You
can't look like a car salesman. You have to have the suit, the red tie,
and your nails have to be right."

It all sounds so simple—maybe too simple. Eddie gave Wall
Street what it thought it wanted, no question about that. ("It's all
about mutual greed," he says.) But you'd think that after thirty or
forty fallings-out with Eddie, Wall Street would start to catch on.
And the more you hear Wall Street people talk about Eddie's vir-
tues, the more you wonder if some force deeper than greed was at
work. "He's somehow able to connect with you," says a man who
worked with Eddie at Lehman Brothers. "He reaches you." You

wonder if perhaps people on Wall Street didn't look at Eddie and recognize themselves. Eddie is a little package of attitudes commonly held but seldom voiced in the world of money. In his distorted and lovable way, Eddie is a caricature of Modern Financial Man.

Eddie says he learned his trade at Lehman Brothers in 1971. That is at once true and unfair to Lehman. He didn't start out at Lehman Brothers and didn't spend much more time at Lehman than he did elsewhere. He started in 1968 at a firm called Bruns, Nordeman, with whom his father had kept his brokerage account until his death in 1964. Herman Braverman, who ran a corset shop in Brooklyn, made his real fortune—of about $250,000—speculating in the stock market in the 1950s. Herman's broker, Otto Kahn, gave Eddie his first job. "Even as a kid he was a con artist," says Kahn. "His father used to come in and say how smart little Eddie was, because he could always fool the adults." Two years after he hired Eddie, Kahn was told by the head office of Bruns, Nordeman, to fire Eddie for what it considered slippery dealings with customers. That is what led Eddie to Lehman Brothers, which was indeed the seminal move of his career.

He lasted only five months before he was fired. The story is still told by stockbrokers about how Eddie found a gun and chased after the sales manager who fired him from Lehman. And it is true that the three men who jointly decided that Eddie had to go spent a few hours in hiding when they heard the rumor that Eddie was armed and loose on Wall Street. But Eddie's crime of choice wasn't murder; it was deception. His weapon wasn't a gun but a telephone. "The gun," it turned out, was a water pistol. Far more dangerous— and what should have concerned the Lehman sales managers—was the batch of big names and the thin handbook that Eddie took with him when he left Lehman. The names—Billy Welsh, Lew Glucksman, Pete Peterson—were for dropping. Eddie is fond of saying things like "Lew Glucksman taught me table manners in the Lehman Brothers boardroom." (Glucksman, a trader not noted for his table manners, laughs and says, "He must be kidding.") The handbook was titled *The Lehman Brothers Sales Technique*.

Eddie almost single-handedly turned the Lehman handbook into Wall Street's official textbook on stockbrokering. He knew in his bones that there were two sides of Wall Street. On one side were firms such as Lehman Brothers, which had the time and the resources to create training manuals; on the other were dozens of low-budget brokerage firms that peddled shares in unlisted, financially strapped companies to anyone who didn't hang up on them twice.

What Eddie did was a bit like giving nuclear weapons to a fundamentalist Third World nation. The SEC has taken to calling the small firms in which Eddie spent most of his career "boiler room operations," but the brokers who work inside call them chop houses. A chop house is less a productive enterprise than a parody of a productive enterprise. The very existence of the company in which they were selling shares was often a matter of semantics. "It didn't matter what the company did," says Eddie, "because investors aren't interested in the company. They're interested in making money." The job of the chop house was to make the company seem like a much better investment than it was. The process was a sustained illusion, a Potemkin village of investment advice. The chop house might well have consisted of only a few grubby square feet of linoleum on which Brooklyn boys peddled shares in companies nobody had heard of; it might have opened and shut in six months. But everything about it was tailored to suggest that it wasn't all that different from Morgan Stanley.

Starting with its name: pick any name remotely connected with permanence, and the odds are it has found its way into the yellow pages under "Investment Services." Buckingham Securities was one, now defunct. Versailles Securities is another. The list reads like a guide to European monuments—either that or the Philadelphia Social Register. Eddie himself once started a firm called Mitchell, White, and Duveen, in which none of the employees was named either Mitchell, White, or Duveen. Eddie, like all good con artists, understood the art of illusion.

He understood it so well that he was paid to teach it to chop house brokers. "All of these places need a man who can take their sales force and put them on a coordinated program," says Michael Hsu, who hired Eddie as his sales manager at A. L. Havens. "There are enough of these shops that are desperate," says Hsu. "They might be about to go out of business. They don't have much to lose."

Eddie has repeated the contents of his handbook so often that he can recite long passages from memory. Young brokers across Wall Street first learned what it meant to sell stocks by watching Eddie do just this. He put himself on a speakerphone and took young brokers right through a Lehman Brothers sales call—or at least what he *said* was a Lehman Brothers sales call.

He began with the faux-sincere greeting: "Let's be candid with each other. You probably know that we at Windsor Court make a lot of money for our customers. . . ." He taught brokers to train their customers to obey. ("You learn a lot about the American people by watching Eddie," says a broker who sat beside him. "They're sheep.") "Did you ever go to the track?" Eddie would ask his customers, with a winning smile. "Sometimes you have to bet on the jockey and not on the horse." He taught brokers how to overcome objections. "There are only forty-one reasons why people won't buy stock from you," he explained. And the Lehman handbook had a phrase for every one of them. If the man on the other end of the phone claimed he had no money to invest, a new young broker could simply turn to page four and read: "Don't you agree that most people will find the money to buy the things they really want? Let's start small with a $10,000 trade. . . ." Occasionally the customer insisted on having information about a company before buying its shares. Imagine! The broker might counter: "If I drove a 1990 Rolls-Royce into your driveway and told you it would cost you ten grand, would you ask me for a report or would you say, 'Sold!'?"

The small firms in which much of Eddie's career unfolded drew on a common pool of talent. Chop house brokers are nomads. The chop house folds or is shut down by the SEC, and its employees move on in a teeming, peristaltic mass. Eddie set up a headhunting business on the side to help the people he trained move along to new jobs: "Eddie Braverman's traveling band of troubadours," as one broker who worked with Eddie calls the operation. What keeps them working, very often, is the need to pay off debts. "The guys who produced," says a young broker who worked with Eddie at Steven Andrew, "were the ones with horse racing debts who were afraid of having their legs broken"—guys like Eddie.

Given this sort of pressure to perform, it's almost forgivable that Eddie occasionally squeezed his customers. The beginning of

Eddie's squeeze was a warm embrace, from which the victim could slither if he wished. Eddie told small investors that he could take a little of their money and turn it into a lot: wealth without risk, gain without toil. In other words, he told people what they wanted to believe but knew they shouldn't. Eddie was Temptation personified. The chop house stockbroker, Eddie says, "is selling wishes and dreams." Wellshire Securities was Eddie's last chop house and is as good a place as any to illustrate what he means by this.

Like many of Eddie's employers, Wellshire specialized in the shares of a single company, an equipment-leasing concern called Ventura. Ventura wasn't an easy sale, even for Eddie. As he says, "The company we were selling [Ventura] didn't exist. It was just a piece of paper." What's more, Eddie wasn't even registered with the NASD to sell. He pitched investors and then put another broker, named Joe Jenkins, on the line to mop up. "I would get them so excited," says Eddie with a smile, "that the sale was basically closed." Then what? "Then Jenkins would come on and say, 'I have a present to give you, and let's just keep it between ourselves.'" The "present" was shares in Ventura.

Working from what he refers to as "the handbook of million-aires," Eddie cold-called potential investors to tell them about Ventura. Eddie eased them into Ventura slowly. "The idea," says Eddie, "was to get them [the investors] to buy a real stock, like AT&T, and then convert it into Ventura." For a time it seemed like a good idea. "They were able to talk doctors into giving them $20,000," says Brian Smith, who worked beside them. "They'd tell customers, 'We're going to get the stock up five bucks in three weeks because we're going to control the flow.'" The fees were fat, even by Wall Street's standards. "Guys would invest $4,000, and Braverman and Jenkins would take $700 in commission," says Smith. The day came, however, when everyone wanted to sell at once. The bubble burst. "Customers started calling to complain they'd been given shares they hadn't bought," Smith says. And only then did it occur to anyone that something was wrong.

The twenty years Eddie spent on Wall Street appear, to the casual observer, to have been a mission to separate investors from their savings. His occasional assignments in more reputable firms weren't any more philanthropic than his more frequent ones in the chop houses. For example, one of the upscale stops on Eddie's itinerary was Dean Witter. In 1987, shortly after Eddie left, the firm received a letter from a Dr. Seymour Leiner. Leiner had opened an account with Eddie in late 1986; he was writing to explain that Eddie had made unauthorized trades in the account. It turned out Eddie had bought a few stocks in Leiner's name that were news to Leiner. "We subsequently started receiving margin calls and overnight letters on almost a daily basis," wrote Leiner, "which he informed my wife were to be discarded, and no attention was to be paid to them. He continually recommended that we convert the equity on our house into the stock market since he was doing so well for us, contrary to what was shown on the monthly statements."

There were at least two more complaints about Eddie during his brief stay at Dean Witter, both from doctors. Dr. Donald Chu wrote to the SEC in September 1987 that Eddie had bought shares in his account without asking him. Dr. Ian Kellman wrote to NASD that his wife had opened an account at Dean Witter and sent money to Eddie, telling him it was to be used for her children's education and not to be put at risk. "He agreed," wrote Kellman, "and said he would deal in blue-chip stocks only. My wife then directed him to purchase stock for her at his discretion, agreeing to invest approximately $3,000 in the market at that time. Mr. Braverman called my wife back and said he had bought almost $14,000 worth of stock because the market was going up." Dr. Kellman later discovered that "we had intended to purchase approximately $28,000 worth of stock and found ourselves on the line for almost $60,000."

Three snapshots from the file on Eddie at the NASD don't begin to do justice to his special talent to deceive. Many stockbrokers have had their way with doctors. Where Eddie really distinguished himself was by fleecing his employers with equal ease. He picked the pockets of some of the world's most pocket-sensitive people. The court documents reveal that Eddie left owing $32,000 to Lehman Brothers (1978); $350 to E. F. Hutton (1978); $49,800 to Rooney, Pace (1985), of which $43,000 was damages paid to Eddie's customers; $6,800 to PaineWebber; $3,400 to Bailey, Martin & Appel (1986); and $9,500 to Dean Witter (1987). Many, many others—including Haas Securities, Berkeley Securities, Mostel & Taylor, and Wertheim—claim that Eddie still owes them money. As a manager at Wertheim put it, "He had no guilt, no sense of remorse. He owed us money when we fired him, and *he* took *us* to small-claims court. The case was thrown out."

There is no more compliant victim of fraud than a Wall Street firm. A Wall Street firm would generally rather write off a few thousand dollars and try to forget the name of Eddie Braverman than have its name mixed up in a public scandal. So there's no telling how long Eddie could have kept this up if he had limited his games to Wall Street. For some reason, however, he assumed that people off Wall Street would be as indulgent of his games as people on Wall Street; that was his big mistake.

Unlike a lot of people, Eddie wasn't able to behave one way at work and another at home. His private life was as mendacious as his professional life, and the two often overlapped. When he left a chop house in 1986 and joined Dean Witter, Eddie moved to a small town in Pennsylvania near the three doctors he would later exploit. The doctors came to consider him a friend. Looking back on it, however, they say they could see that Eddie was headed for a fall. There was something not quite right about him.

For instance, Eddie had arrived in town without a stick of furniture. How many forty-two-year-old Wall Street stockbrokers travel like a Swede on summer vacation? "He only had two things," recalls one of the doctors' wives. "He had a big mirror from his mother's house and an oil painting of himself." But the main thing that caught her attention was that wherever Eddie went, a line of creditors wasn't far behind. Every check Eddie wrote bounced, from the big one for the champagne-color Porsche to the small one for the dog to replace the one that his wife had taken during one of the many times she left Eddie for good.

The dogs were another clue. Eddie seemed to have taken to heart the old Wall Street saw that if you want a friend, you should buy a dog. Eddie had a fetish for West Highland terriers and had owned several, all of which he named Tibby. There were almost as many exotic stories about the Tibbys as there were about Eddie. Tibby I had been kidnapped at gunpoint by a tile man to whom Eddie had written and bounced a check. Tibby II had its back leg broken by another of Eddie's creditors. Tibby III was suspended out of the window of one of Eddie's apartments by yet a third creditor. The stories sound like the desperate inventions of a vaudeville hack. But they ring true to people who know Eddie. "The only thing that was honest about Ed," says the minister who baptized him, "was his love for his dogs. His creditors might have known they would have gotten a more positive response than if they hung his wife out the window." Says one of his creditors: "I think the dogs are in on it."

By the time Eddie reached Dean Witter, Tibby II was on his last leg, and Eddie had bounced more checks than most people write in a lifetime. Most brokers grow richer the longer they stay on Wall Street. Eddie just bounced larger and larger checks. One of the many judges who have looked down from the bench upon Eddie's smiling face described him as "a professional check-bouncer." Gas stations, furniture stores, moving companies, car dealers, landlords, real estate brokers, the Internal Revenue Service, even his own lawyers were after Eddie for money, which explains Eddie's reluctance to stay in one place: from Great Neck to Manhattan, from Manhattan to Brooklyn, from Brooklyn to Great Neck, around and around he went.

You could tell that Eddie had moved into your building by the line of large men in muscle shirts forming at the front desk. They were not uniformly nice. Last year, while he was living on East 43rd Street, Eddie bounced a check for more than a thousand dollars to a retailer of fine Italian menswear, the kind of place that sells jet set ties and makes all its customers look sharp, the kind of place you just don't bounce a check to. But Eddie did. And every day for a couple of weeks a large man parked himself outside Eddie's building and waited for him. He said he was "a friend" of the man at the Italian clothing store. He said his name was Joey. "Let me tell you about Joey," says the manager of the Italian menswear store. "My friend Joey is a real bent-nose kind of guy. Lemme tell ya. When Joey is angry—when Joey is only a little bit angry—you don't *even* want to know him." The doorman at the International Plaza on 43rd Street still hasn't recovered. "He bounced checks to everyone in the neighborhood," says the doorman, "right down to one for $1.27 for cigarettes. He was crazy."

He was. *That* was what was wrong with Eddie; that was why he was headed for a fall. Somewhere in his complex pathology was a wide streak of narcissism. Head doctors who have worked on and around the Street see it often. "What I notice in many of the brokers I see," says Manhattan psychologist Mari Terzaghi, "is that through work they are regaining a sense of omnipotence that they once had in childhood. Many of these people are narcissistic and treat other people as need-satisfying objects. They feel as though they deserve to take."

The inside of Eddie's head could fill a textbook. You can imagine a psychiatrist ticking off the chart with one hand and reaching for the phone to call his publisher with the other as Eddie lies back and begins to talk about himself. Eddie was forever complaining about his life-threatening case of hepatitis: hypochondria (1). Eddie felt everyone was out to get him (and they were): paranoia (2). When Eddie traveled he carried only a mirror and a large oil painting of himself; when he wrote checks for cash he wrote them to "Myself": self-obsession (3). Eddie needed to feel big. He'd boast of making hundreds of thousands of dollars, even when explaining to a judge in small claims court why he couldn't repay a loan of a few hundred dollars: grandiosity (4). Eddie craved any sort of attention. Most Wall Street brokers spread rumors and malicious gossip about other people. Eddie spread rumors and malicious gossip about himself: weird grandiosity (4a). Eddie's only real friends were dogs: you figure it out (5). And in spite of it all, Eddie was so very charming, so painfully charming, you wanted to like him as much as he wanted to like himself; and at the same time you didn't really understand *why* you wanted so much to like him. In his essay on narcissism Freud wrote that "the charm of the child is to a great extent his narcissism." So many people told me that Eddie reminded them of "a little boy" that I began to wonder if the charm of the narcissist wasn't to a great extent a child's.

What's interesting about all this is that none of it mattered when it came time for Eddie's next job interview. If Eddie was crazy, it was in a way Wall Street understood. In his twenty years as a stockbroker, Eddie only once received a warning about his rubber checkbook. On Christmas Eve in 1980 the New York Stock Exchange wrote to say that "in the exchange's view the issuance of insufficient-funds checks by a registered representative for any purpose is reprehensible conduct." If he did it again, he'd be in big trouble. He did it again a hundred times, and no one ever seems to have held it against him.

Until recently,* as the eighties waned, the SEC began to look at the small fish as well as the big fish. In August 1988 the Securities and Exchange Commission approved rules to make it more difficult for brokers like Eddie to sell. Then came a flurry of cases by the SEC against the chop houses, including a place called Haas Securities. Haas was shut down for unscrupulous sales practices. Earlier in his career Eddie had spent a few happy months training the stockbrokers at Haas to sell.

All along he stayed at least one step ahead of the law. When I called the SEC in February, I was told there was no disciplinary file on Edward Braverman. A spokesman said he was just another broker with a clean record. Then, in March, the SEC issued the following press release:

> The Securities and Exchange Commission said it filed a civil complaint in U.S. District Court against Wellshire Securities; Robert Cohen, its president; Carol Martino, executive vice president; Joseph Jenkins, a broker; Edward Braverman, a former Wellshire broker; and Alan Diamond, Wellshire's former trader. . . . The commission alleged that from June 1988 to the present Wellshire operated as a penny-stock boiler room. The complaint alleges that Wellshire employees made exorbitant and baseless prices, predictions, and other materially false and misleading statements in selling securities.

Eddie wasn't available to be handcuffed. He had lasted only three months at Wellshire. The trouble began only a few weeks after he began to peddle shares in Ventura. He started showing up late for work. Then he began disappearing into a back room of the office in the middle of the workday. Brian Smith was asked to watch the door while he did his business, which Smith says involved "big rubber bands, a candle, and a burnt-out old can." A couple of weeks later Eddie appeared at Wellshire with cut marks across his face. "He said

*In 1990

he'd done it shaving," says Smith, "but nobody is that bad with a razor." And at last—as ever—he began to borrow money from his fellow brokers. Bad debts led inexorably to the unfortunate incident in which he was dangled by a fellow broker from an eleventh-story window. (Steve Jenkins, Wellshire broker and brother of Joe, confirms this happened, though he's vague on the altitude. When asked if Eddie was in fact eleven stories off the ground, he grows impatient. "Howda I know?" he says. "I'm notta arckiteck.") Finally, last October, Eddie wrote one too many bad checks to local merchants. The police who came to haul Eddie away to face the charges wore rubber gloves, as if to dispose of toxic waste.

This Eddie Braverman story ended on a particularly haunting note, however. As Eddie was hustled out the door, Wellshire checked to see what was missing. Sure enough, the firm found Eddie had taken a $14,000 Corvette with him. Eddie had charged the car to the credit card of Robert Cohen, Wellshire's president, and somehow had never gotten around to paying him back. It was a safe bet that Eddie was broke—between the wife and the drugs, Eddie was always broke—so the question became how to retrieve the Corvette. Brian Smith volunteered to resteal it, in exchange for a collection fee of $5,000.

Smith knew Eddie well. He decided to set a trap. "His weakness is money," says Smith. "So I called him up and said, 'Eddie, I know you're short on cash. Come and pick me up from work and give me a lift home, and I'll spot you $300.'" Eddie agreed and fetched Smith from Wellshire's front door. On the drive from Manhattan to Long Island they stopped for gas. When Eddie left the car to pay the attendant, Smith drove away, simple as that. But that wasn't the haunting bit. The haunting bit was what Eddie had said when Brian Smith offered to lend him money. As he already owed money to Smith—and about ten thousand other people—he should have been surprised. Another man might have said, "What's the catch?" or at least, "That's kind of you." Not Eddie. Eddie said, "Yeah, yeah. Good idea. You owe me." *You owe me.* "His whole mind-set is that way," says Smith. "Everybody owes him."

You can hear a lot of what has happened on Wall Street in those three words: *You owe me.* You can hear a chorus of twenty-five-year-olds complaining that their six-figure bonuses aren't big enough. You can hear bond salesmen building in their bigger-than-life fees. You can hear Bruce Wasserstein and Eric Gleacher baring their souls to Henry Kravis before the buyout of RJR Nabisco: "Henry, we've been thinking about it, and we've decided we should be paid $50 million for this deal." You can hear the voice of an entire culture based on entitlement. Eddie merely put the words to the music. Of course Eddie was different from the big names on Wall Street. (If he weren't he would never have actually said what he did.) Eddie never had his picture on the cover of *Business Week*.

Eddie now lives in rural Pennsylvania, blissfully unaware that the SEC is after him and that the NASD has at last banned him from the brokerage industry. (Not that this matters. As one senior Wall Street person says, "There are whole firms comprised exclusively of people who have been banned from the industry.") When I finally caught up with him, he was standing trial for passing bad checks in Newtown, Pennsylvania. Anyone who has seen Eddie's file in the Bucks County Courthouse will feel they know Newtown before they arrive, for there is hardly a store in the place that hasn't filed a suit against him. The Sunoco station, Barry's Furniture, the Hoover market, Texaco, Camera Craft, and the Acme market each had one of Eddie's checks pinned to its cash register.

For his part, Eddie remains decidedly upbeat, more irritated than troubled by the charges he faces. "Pennsylvania," he says, "is not part of America. That's why they call it a commonwealth instead of a state. What they're doing to me is undemocratic." Eddie looks forward to getting back to Wall Street. "The more they publicize me," he says, "the easier it will be for me to do my job. Whatever you write about me, positive or negative, will help my career."

In only one respect could Eddie be called a changed man. He recently became a Christian. Eddie was baptized in Newtown by a minister we'll call Edwards at a church we'll call St. Mark's. It happened much as you might expect by now. Eddie needed money. He attended services for two consecutive Sundays and then introduced himself. "One of the first things he told me," says Edwards, "was that Jesus would save him. He said, 'I'm Jewish, but I had a conversion experience while I was in the hospital. I prayed to Jesus and I got well.'" St. Mark's, as it happens, kept a kitty to help people get back on their feet. While asking to be baptized out of one side of his mouth, Eddie asked for a loan out of the other. Over a couple of months Edwards lent him several thousand dollars. He was impressed by Eddie's "constant tales of woe."

The minister, since, has come to doubt the sincerity of Eddie's conversion. And the money was never returned. "When he said he couldn't repay the money," recalls Edwards, "he said he would invest $1,000 for me in the stock market and make it double. Now I don't believe in easy gain to start with. Not that I think it's evil, I just don't think it happens." How unlike the times that sounds.

Bulldog Bull

Paul Volcker had agreed to give the keynote address at the tenth anniversary of the Yale School of Organization and Management (SOM). The hall was jammed with alums. "All of a sudden people began to applaud," says Joan Ryan, director of public relations. "All of a sudden they began to stand. People in the audience were weeping and crying." Volcker asked the dean what was going on. It was a spontaneous outburst, he was told, that had nothing to do with him. Tears of joy flowed because the Yale School of Management lived on. "That's just the way we are at SOM," says Ryan. "We're different."

True enough, it's not exactly what you'd expect from a business school reunion. But perhaps even more unusual is how I happened upon this anecdote. It wasn't through diligent legwork or shrewd questioning. Rather, it was spoon-fed to me over the phone as I lay in bed trying to sleep. Just hours after I had mentioned to a Yale student that I would be writing this article, I received a call from the SOM public relations office, intent on telling me about the emotional depth of its alumni.

Yale believes it plays a special role in the education of America's managers. "Students get everything they can get from a conventional school plus some," says acting Dean Joe Peck. When Yale people talk about "conventional schools," they usually mean Harvard. "Our people can make a profit with the best of them, but they also want a happy workplace," says Ryan. "SOM draws people with a passion about things. It's a mission-based institution," says a student.

Yalies throw around the word "mission" quite a bit. Were you to wander the halls of the Harvard Business School and randomly ask, "What is your mission?" students would assume you were some flakeball who lost his way to a divinity school pep rally. At Yale, by comparison, this is an almost natural way to start a conversation. "What is your mission?" I cryptically asked total strangers. Everyone knew exactly what I was talking about, and no one laughed except one student who said the mission was "to land on Mars." Then even he got serious.

The Yale School of Management's mission is poignant enough to move grownups to tears, but vague enough to elude a generally accepted definition. A part of it, all agree, is that Yale trains managers for both the private and the public sectors, while other business schools produce more run-of-the-mill captains of industry. While the big issue at Harvard is whether graduates will make their millions by building better widgets in Ohio or by leeching on Wall Street, Yale brows furrow over whether students should make their millions at all. Students are meant to be driven by values more noble than greed. This supposedly reflects the intentions of the founding fathers: investment banker William Donaldson, Yale president Kingman Brewster, philanthropist and businessman William Beinecke, and Yale professor of economics John Perry Miller. "In my 30-odd years in business," said Beinecke in a speech called "The Birth of the School," "few things have surprised and disappointed me more than the attitude many businessmen have about the world. . . . Even men of the highest capacity will, without regret, limit themselves to a two-course curriculum—they major in the bottom line and minor in golf." Yale would not send "its students into the world with wrong, distorted, overly self-serving values for living their lives."

Pretty noble stuff, but what does it mean in practice? "We're trying to be everything good at once," says marketing professor K. Sridhar Moorthy, in discussing how Yale markets its newest professional school. Leafing through a Yale School of Management p. r. package, one finds an incredible number of boasts (even for a p. r. package), some of which seem mutually exclusive. Yale promotes good citizenship. Yale promotes entrepreneurship. Yale trains managers for *both* the private and the public sectors. Yale concentrates on *both* research and teaching. Yale is a cooperative rather than a competitive environment, which is why Yale has a relaxed grading system and elects no class officers. Yet Yale provides a rigorous education and places graduates with the most prestigious Wall Street firms, and so on.

Who says you can't have it all? But the student of Yale's dreams probably doesn't exist. If she did (and it would be a woman, since Yale prides itself on having more women than any conventional business school), she would be an investment banker who quit, say, Goldman Sachs to enter SOM. She applies only to SOM, because only SOM offers the curriculum she seeks. In her first year she finds a more efficient way to distribute fire stations in her hometown of Washington, D.C. She resists the advances of Bain & Co. and spends her summer creating a Big Brother/Big Sister program on the South Side of Chicago. Upon graduating she eschews a million-dollar offer from Salomon Brothers and instead goes to work at $35,000 per annum for the Congressional Budget Office. In short order she balances the federal budget and at the same time increases the generosity of all social welfare programs. She moonlights as a concert pianist, giving her performances in poor neighborhoods at no charge. She refuses many calls from headhunters to remain in the public sector. Interviewed by the *Wall Street Journal,* she thanks Yale for giving her the management tools and the values to do her job. Oh yes—somewhere she finds several hundred million dollars and donates it to the Yale School of Organization and Management.

Regardless of what it actually graduates, the school dearly wants to be thought to produce a certain kind of superachieving altruist and does not take kindly to reporters who show up and ask how many of their graduates took jobs with investment banks last year (25 percent). "Sometimes we get a hard-nosed reporter who looks only at the numbers," said Mrs. Ryan from public relations with a frown. A hard-nosed article in *Business Week* last November showed that though half of the SOM Class of 1986 came from the public sector, only 15 percent returned there. SOMers respond to these figures in three ways. First, they say that Yalies are in private sector jobs with a public sector flavor. They may be on Wall Street, for example, but they work in public finance. They also say that Yalies will return to the public sector after they pay off the $40,000 of debt they have accumulated while at Yale. Or finally, like Nancy Bove, the director of placement at SOM, they might say, "I don't think that [placing graduates in the public sector] was ever part of the mission." The school is nevertheless cobbling together a loan forgiveness program and an internship fund for students who go into public sector jobs.

An even more sensitive issue than what students should be when they grow up is what students are taught in class. Yale has stressed a discipline called Organizational Behavior (OB)—of course, not to the exclusion of more conventional subjects such as economics, finance, and accounting. (At SOM nothing is ever to the exclusion of anything else.) Economists, unfortunately, tend to look down their noses at OBs (just as physicists look down their noses at economists). OB is a "softer" social science. OBs and economists have entirely different notions about what motivates people and therefore some pretty different ideas about how to manage them. "We're satisficers rather than optimisers," says OB program head Victor Vroom. SOM was built around the OB department, and some OB professors regard SOM's slow but steady acquisition of economics and finance departments as selling the "mission" down river. "We've hired a number of people who would like us to be another University of Chicago," says Vroom. He means: strip Yale of its social conscience and turn everyone into Milton Friedman.

"If I were a mad economist, and I wanted to get rid of your department, how would I start?" I asked Vroom, just for fun.

"Get rid of community-building," said Vroom.

Community-building is to the Yale School of Management what the first night holding hands around the campfire is to an Outward Bound program or the first shared prayer to a religious retreat. It certainly sets the place apart from conventional schools. All new students meet in a room. Vroom asks them to pair off with someone they don't know and to learn about each other. He then confronts the pair and challenges them to dig down deep. "This person is a living, breathing human being," he says. "You have one minute to think of a way to find out more about him than superficial facts."

Community-building occurs as the newly acquainted pair finds another pair. Then the foursome finds another foursome. Eight people form a group that then makes itself even more uncomfortable. For example, Vroom asks all members of the group to relate their honest first impressions of everyone else and to say which person makes them most and least comfortable. The group then takes an OB course called Individual and Group Behavior together. "Years later at reunions you see the groups reassemble," says Vroom. "It is a tremendously powerful bonding exercise."

Yale is clearly no place for people uncomfortable in crowds. And since I had always thought of entrepreneurs as strong-headed loners, like Steve Jobs, I wondered how Yale could lay claim to producing an entrepreneurial spirit. What's more, as members of an anointed elite, SOM graduates pay a high opportunity cost if they choose to strike out on their own. Virtually every Wall Street investment bank interviews on the SOM campus. "We have a problem with [the seductiveness of] 25-year-old investment bankers in Armani suits rolling up in limos," says placement director Bove. It is a problem familiar even to conventional schools. But the Yale brochure with a wave of the semantic wand settles the matter: "Some entrepreneurs find opportunity in their own businesses; some give new direction to an established business; some provide creative management in the public and non-profit sectors." At Yale we can all be entrepreneurs.

But being everything good at once is only half of the SOM mission. It is also important to avoid being anything bad. Ivan Boesky, we can now all agree, is bad. But at one time he was featured in the SOM admissions brochure. Upon his arrest, his picture was removed. Then an interesting thing happened: Yale seemed to realize that what was bad for Boesky could be good for Yale. Wasn't this the message of the founding fathers? Greed was on the way out, and public service might, just might, be on the way back in. A seminal article, now part of Yale's public relations kit, appeared in the *Yale Alumni Magazine* called "No Boeskys, Please." "Among the staff of the School of Organization and Management," reports the article, "there is a palpable sense of relief that an offer by Boesky to give a lecture series was refused" (whew, that was a close one!). A student named Chris Koller says, "Everyone was thrilled he got caught."

"We try to admit good citizens," the director of admissions, Richard Silverman, told me. Hence the title of the alumni magazine article. Students hold a majority of seats on the SOM admissions committee and prevent future Boeskys from getting in. Last spring, according to the article, students

> played a key role in turning away at least one highly quali-
> fied applicant. The man had good grades and high GMAT
> scores. He had been captain of a college athletic team and
> had distinguished himself working for a prominent Wall
> Street firm. That firm, however, had been in the news in
> connection with a check kiting scandal.

Clearly this was E. F. Hutton. Guilt by association? Well, the article quotes SOM's former dean, Burton Malkiel, explaining: "The admissions committee did not admit him because when he talked about his experience, the kinds of things he was doing, and his likes, he didn't mention what they thought should have been his shame about the kinds of things going on in the firm."

As far as I could make out, SOM students are uniformly good citizens. They don't stick gum under the tables in their cafeteria, and I searched the toilet stalls in vain for a word of graffiti. They are obsessed by their school. And, it is true, SOMers seem to have a genuine concern for public welfare, even if they do end up selling options at Salomon Brothers for a living. Last winter, without pay, Yale students figured out how to snowplow the streets of New Haven more efficiently than it has ever been done before. You can find this information too in your p. r. package.

But even if they want to devote their lives to doing good works, SOMers find no natural course to follow upon graduation. There is no elite civil service in America as there is in England and France. They're all dressed up with no place to go. They are waiting for their Jack Kennedy, in a sense, to restore the pride in government service or perhaps for another depression to decrease the attractiveness of the private sector. In its relations with the real world, Yale seems to feel backed into a corner and is becoming excessively concerned with its image. I am willing to accept the possibility of a rare breed of elite altruists. But I am wary of self-advertised elite altruists. When hyping the mission is such a big part of the mission, it's hard not to get suspicious.

Mary Cunningham,
Meet Ward Cleaver

You know the American Century isn't over yet—indeed, that it's making something of a comeback—when you see people on the street who remind you of Ward Cleaver. Ward Cleaver was the father of Wally and Beaver on the 1950s television show *Leave It to Beaver;* he was the embodiment of solid, middle-American, 1950s values. He went to church without being preachy, put bread on the table without grubbing for money, did community service without seeming superior, stayed married to his wife without cheating, and raised his children to be just like him. I assumed I'd never see anything like him again once I started watching *Star Trek* on a rival channel. But I was wrong. I've just met the Harvard business school class of 1979. Even though they are filthy rich (25 percent are already millionaires), they are more like Ward Cleaver than most people I know. The women are too.

When the Harvard B-school class of 1979 celebrated its tenth reunion, I didn't go for a number of good reasons—like I'm not an alum. But I had some of my people there. The only stir was created by Mary Cunningham (HBS '79) and her husband, Bill Agee. Agee was CEO of Bendix when it was devoured by Martin Marietta. Cunningham was Agee's nubile assistant and swears in her book, *Powerplay,* that she *did not* sleep with her boss while the two of them were putting Bendix out of business. She was only "mentored" by him.

Anyway, Agee turned up at the HBS black-tie dinner and

dance wearing a neon lime green jacket. As others stared in disbelief, he twirled Mary into a corner of the dance floor. "I couldn't be sure," says one source, "but I believe they were mentoring each other." Otherwise it was a normal affair—the reunion, I mean. The class nodded through lectures with titles such as "The Competitive Advantage of Nations." Awards were given to "outstanding alumni," i.e. graduates who had donated big bucks to HBS. There was a dinner and two lunches. Then everyone went home.

Before they left, however, they were handed a book. To this volume 312 members (42 percent) of the class had contributed photographs and five-hundred-word summaries of their lives and ambitions. Judging from these, John Shad is wasting the $20 million he's donating to create an ethics program at the business school. It's almost as if the crumbling of all-American values, the upheavals of the 1960s and early 1970s in which most of the class of 1979 came of age, had never happened. HBSers, who stuck to capitalism when times were tough, are breathing a collective sigh of relief: "Whew! Sure glad all that consciousness-raising is over!" Or, as one member writes, "George Bush is right: 'Don't worry, be happy!' "

American Centurions: it was their pictures that first put me in mind of Ward Cleaver. Well-groomed couples stand smiling over broods of children. They all look alike. Any child in the book could belong to any HBS parent. I then read their descriptions of their lives. They all *sound* alike. Any five-hundred-word profile could belong to any HBS graduate. Leafing through the book, you begin to get a sense of, well, standards—very 1950s. It's possible that there are in the 1980s, somewhere in the world, groups of more like-minded adults (Moonies, for example, or professional race walkers), but I haven't met them. I've got to travel backward thirty years in my mind to find such homogeneity.

But when all is said and done, these are *not* the Cleavers, because when you put your ear up close to the pages of this remarkable book you hear sounds that almost existed in America thirty years ago, but not quite. Listen. HBSers reflecting on their pasts:

". . . I survived a high-speed (100 mph) car crash with my wife, . . ." writes a McKinsey consultant. "When we all got home again we very silently made a toast 'to life.' It is amazing how an experience like that crystallizes the mind and makes you realize life is to be enjoyed and you live it only once. . . . Maybe you all know this already, but the trick lies in how you implement it. Hence, after the accident I immediately bought another 911 Turbo. . . ."

". . . The underpinnings of my childhood," says an investment banker, "were rooted in the traditions of nineteenth-century England: a village manor house, public (boarding) school, the British empire. . . ."

And now?

"My aim is to acquire (via LBOs with management) a group of small and medium-sized companies. . . ."

"As much as I enjoyed working at McDonald's," says a currency trader with Continental Grain, "I wanted to realize a lifelong dream to trade as a speculator, for profit. . . . My only regret is that I didn't start speculating earlier."

Hear it? The American Centurions tend to sprinkle their conversation with platitudes, just as Ward Cleaver did. ("Now, Beaver, it's wrong to borrow money you can't repay.") From the tone of these you can tell the B-School class of 1979 holds many firm beliefs too. But they aren't quite the same firm beliefs:

"Stay liquid," says a class of 1979 real estate mogul.

"Get entrepreneurial before you have children," says a man who has just finished laying an optical fiber on the ocean floor.

". . . Being innocent victims of alleged white-collar crimes is both time-consuming and costly to correct," says a former treasurer of Jiffy Lube International who is depicted wearing one of those cone-head party hats much favored by the Cleavers on birthdays.

Since the 1950s both marital fidelity and the amount of time parents spend with their children have waned. But you'd never know it from meeting this crowd. Flying in the face of fickle fashion, the members of the class of 1979 are straining to place the interests of their families above all. But it doesn't quite work out:

"Quality family time is my highest priority," says the cohead of M&A at Smith Barney, "but a heavy travel and work schedule. . . ."

"Although I am still single," says a deal maker with Bear Stearns, "it is not by choice, and I am constantly on the lookout for the right opportunity."

"I am . . . divorced," admits one investment banker.

". . . divorced again," says a second.

The twelve lines in each profile marked "Activities" are particularly revealing. I've never actually met anyone who has twelve lines' worth of activities, but quite a few members of the class of 1979 manage to consume the space. Skeptics will say that the only constructive activity that goes on at the Harvard business school is résumé building, that HBSers sound more like college applicants with low SAT scores than fully grown adults. Those skeptics obviously haven't read this book. It describes a group of people almost committed to making the world around them a better place to live.

"Who's Who in America, Phi Beta Kappa, *Who's Who in Finance"* is the way one banker lists his activities.

Friends of Princeton Sailing, the Union Club, and "keeping up with five newspapers a day," are among a venture capitalist's pastimes.

The Harvard business school class of 1979 is self-effacing. One reason they incline to modesty is that they put the team first; personal glory seems to mean absolutely nothing to them. They recognize, just as patriotic Americans of the 1950s did, that if the team fails, they fail. That is why they are loyal to their employers—well, nearly.

"In work, as in play, I prefer frequent activity and multiple partners," says a partner in a venture-capital company. "Under me at present is my personal assistant, Sandy. If you have seen the movie *Dangerous Liaisons,* you'll know where I'm coming from."

"While my career flourished," says a former airline executive who was almost willing to crash with his company, "Pan Am did not."

In the postwar American spirit, these men and women have grasped that there is no substitute for hard work. In spite of earning more than the vast majority of the population, 89 percent of them put in more than a forty-hour week. Sixteen percent work more than sixty hours, not including commuting time. And a few of them *always* work, even while filling in questionnaires from HBS:

"Should you have a need for coal or know someone who does, please call!" says the vice-president of sales for the Peabody Coal Company.

"By the way, if you don't normally stay at Hyatt when you travel, give us a try," says a marketing man from you know where. "We have clean sheets and good eats. ... . We even have free color TVs in every room!"

"If you need financial backing," says a capitalist, "let me know, and if your idea doesn't get blown away, we'll go with it."

The class of 1979 has a religious streak running through it that is vaguely reminiscent of the comfortable Protestantism of the 1950s. Like the Cleavers, they have reconciled the pursuit of profit with the teachings of the Bible (though for the Cleavers, God was assumed and not waved like a flag).

"If I can share Jesus in any way with you, please let me try," says a sales manager with Philips Circuit Assemblies.

"God willing, I still want to run a large enterprise some day," says a vice-president of a large oil company.

"God blessed me with two good partners," says the millionaire owner of an industrial cleaning company.

"And my ambition?" writes a 3M information-systems manager in Europe. "This is . . . *to serve the purposes of God in my generation.* You may wonder why this doesn't automatically lead to the priesthood or missionary work. This is because the love of the Father must be evident in the workplace as well as those places designated for meeting God."

The industrialists of the Harvard business class of 1979—people who make *things*—have been quicker to find God than the others. The bosses in the engine room of our nation say things like, "I have been blessed" or "I have been fortunate." The investment bankers and the consultants, on the other hand, insist on direct, hands-on control of their fates. Although they form the bulk of the class (McKinsey is the biggest single employer with eleven; Goldman Sachs and Citicorp are tied for second with eight each), not one of them mentions any association with religion.

A cynic might say that with the rise of decision-tree analysis and the hostile takeover, this only makes sense. Why waste time worrying about a Prime Mover when *you* are the Prime Mover? One former Bain & Co. consultant who attended the reunion told me afterward that no Bain consultant, however deeply he believed in God, would ever commit his belief to paper, for fear that his employers would stumble across it and question his devotion to Bain. Me, I prefer the nicer way to look at the evangelism of some HBSers: as something close to a rebirth of those values that made postwar America great. Close, as Ward Cleaver might say, but no cigar.

Franky's
Longest Mile

Let's move ahead to early 1995, when the stock market is weak, junk bonds are strong, and there is yet another mad scramble for leveraged buyout deals. Sherman McCoy is back selling bonds, and Henry Kravis is bidding with management to buy General Motors. Wall Street deal makers are, in short, being paid more than ever. Bruce Wasserstein gives a sinister cackle when asked by the *New York Times* why the eighties have returned to haunt us. "Beware of false endings," he says.

It sounds implausible, like a poltergeist. But is it really any less plausible than the doom of the Wall Street investment banker widely predicted by others? The latest round of funeral preparations was triggered by the collapse of Drexel Burnham Lambert. "So this is the way an era ends . . ." began the cover story of *Business Week*. "A new era has arrived," thumped the cover story in *Time*, which went on to describe a Drexel broker who walked out of his firm, stepped into a waiting limousine, and said, "I'll enjoy reading about all this from Hawaii."

What to make of this seemingly incongruous detail? Merely "one last show of eighties bravado," according to *Time*. Perhaps, but the assertion would have been easier to swallow if the magazine hadn't already voiced it once before. After the 1987 stock market crash, *Time* ran its first epitaph on the age of greed, excess, and bravado. "The tenor of the times will never be the same," it said. Then came the heist of Time, Inc. by Warner, the muddied battle for RJR Nabisco, and a flurry of other seedy deals. The tenor of the times was more hysterical than ever.

It seems that no one can wait to impose his own sense of moral propriety upon the saga of Wall Street in the eighties. You can almost hear journalists thinking as they write: Greedy people always pay the price for their avarice. Or: The proud must fall. That sort of thing. But Wall Street and its people simply do not belong in conventional morality tales. The only moral on Wall Street is that there is no moral.

Let's be cynical, like Wall Street. There was nothing inevitable about the fall of Drexel. The firm had the simple misfortune of owning a pile of bonds that collapsed. Word of its losses leaked to the Street. Then, as it wobbled, another Wall Street investment bank crept up and gave it a push: Salomon Brothers, as *Barron's* revealed, told the Federal Reserve that it was about to announce to the entire bond market that it would no longer do business with Drexel. It was clear that others would follow. Without lines of credit and without government support, Drexel had no choice but to declare bankruptcy.

Now, it is true that God works in mysterious ways. But no one has ever accused him of rigging the bond market. With a bit more trading luck and a bit more trading guile, Drexel could well have looked forward to playing the leading role in the resurgence of the junk bond market in 1992. It may be true, as the newspapers said, that Drexel got only what it deserved. If so, it was a fluky stroke of justice. In the United States greedy people don't get what they deserve. They get rich.

What is more, nothing in Drexel's failure signals the end of an era. There is no sign that anyone on Wall Street has been chastened by Drexel's ordeal. A few days after Drexel's collapse, a visitor to Morgan Stanley found the managing directors squabbling over a batch of small, trendy cellular phones that had just arrived at the firm. Of course all of them already had phones in their briefcases. But that wasn't enough. They all absolutely had to have the *smaller* phones. Meanwhile, Drexel's own bosses were still focused on their bank accounts, having paid themselves bonuses that would have made executives of solvent companies blush.

When the end came, the first addition to Drexel's offices at 60

Broad Street was a bevy of security guards hired to search the staff as they left. Despite this, the first reaction on the Drexel trading floor was to grab anything that wasn't nailed down. "Computers and fax machines were definitely walking out the door," says one employee. No doubt they'll be put to good use. All of Wall Street is combing the ruins in search of Drexel deal makers who can make them rich. And Merrill Lynch and others have already hinted about their desire to become the next leader of the junk bond market.

The nineties have no new flavor, partly because they haven't yet gotten under way,* but also because they don't promise to be all that different from the eighties. The raw itch for money is still with us as surely as ever. It supersedes everything. True, the itch has, for the moment, become slightly more difficult for Wall Street to scratch. But money is still status. And the money on the Street is still better than elsewhere. Anyone who doubts this should speak with the three thousand college students who are applying for the eleven financial analyst positions currently offered by Wasserstein Perella & Co. or the seven thousand five hundred college and business school students asking for the six jobs on the trading floor of Salomon Brothers (compared to six thousand for 127 jobs in 1985).

The current Wall Street recession is, in my view, more a technical aberration than a permanent condition in the market. There has been no weakening of the forces that gave birth to the bonanza on Wall Street. Consumers and corporations continue, whenever possible, to borrow money they can't easily repay. The federal tax code still favors debt. The prices of stocks and bonds still gyrate wildly, encouraging speculation in the markets. No one in Washington dares to suggest seriously that short-term gains might be taxed away. Our political leadership still operates on the assumption that anything that is, is right. So "the eighties" on Wall Street will endure, if for no other reason than the inevitability that demand for investment bankers will adjust to meet supply—the junk bond market will recover, yesterday's LBOs will require an overhaul, or the savings and loan bailout will offer new chances to pan gold in the government's coffers.

So how will we know when the era has truly ended? My own

*This piece was written in April 1990.

test is unscientific: monitor the response on Wall Street to criticism from outside. Books and plays such as *Barbarians at the Gate* and *Other People's Money,* which skewer life on the Street, are treated by the Street as rollicking good fun, not to be taken seriously. The Shameless Age is over only when people on Wall Street begin to care what people off Wall Street think.

This doesn't look like it will happen anytime soon. Tom Wolfe was the first to demonstrate how difficult it is for an outsider to insult Wall Street. Just months after the first end of the era, in late 1987, Wolfe's brilliant satire of the bond salesman was being read by everyone who had ever set foot on a trading floor. Dozens of my colleagues at Salomon Brothers, I thought, would be angered or embarrassed by the unveiling and lampooning of the Master of the Universe. I couldn't have been more wrong.

Everyone got the joke except the people it was aimed at. The people I expected to be most wounded were the most inclined to bring it up. They were, if anything, flattered. Their lives were now drama. So it wasn't long before the last trace of irony was drained from memory, and a bond salesman sitting near me celebrated a quick killing by shouting: "I am a Master of the Universe!" Even Sherman wouldn't do that.

Which brings us back to the not-so-small matter of bravado: Have we heard the last, as *Time* suggests, of the outrageous stories that have become the stock-in-trade of the Street? Don't bet on it. Even as I was leafing through *Time,* I got a call from a former colleague at Salomon who had a tale of bravado to tell.

It began with a star Salomon bond trader whom I'll call Franky Simon. One day not so long ago, Franky boasted to a nearby trader that he could run a mile in less than eight minutes. The trader took one look at the putto-like Franky and said he doubted that Franky could run to the elevator if the building were on fire. Franky stood firm. Frankly was a fighter. The argument became a spectacle. A crowd began to gather. The debate raged into Salomon's system-wide loudspeaker—called the Hoot and Holler. Traders and brokers in Chicago, Atlanta, San Francisco, Boston, London, and even Tokyo joined in.

Before long a market was being made in Franky's mile that by the end of the day was 7:30–7:40. (A bet for Franky was that he could run a mile in less than seven minutes and thirty seconds; a bet against him was that he couldn't finish in under seven minutes, forty seconds.) Franky had his doubters. "He used to jog some in college," said a trader who had sold Franky short, "but that was thirty pounds and seven years ago. I thought he could probably run half a mile at that pace. The question was, could he gut out the last quarter mile? I figured he'd collapse." When the betting finished—three hours after it had begun—$8,000 said Franky couldn't beat the clock.

On the other hand, $8,000 said that he could. Chairman and CEO John Gutfreund had laid $500 on Franky. So had Paul Mozer, the managing director and head of government trading, who was Franky's boss. In the words of one trader who had backed Franky, "It's true, he's kind of chubby and soft looking. But you figured he could press it for four laps around the track."

Just to be sure, the traders who had bet on Franky made an investment. They tossed a few hundred dollars to one of Salomon's increasingly rare trainees and told him to find Franky the best running gear money could buy. Franky, with $16,000 riding on him, would fly as never before. The next evening the entire Salomon Brothers trading floor hummed the theme song from *Rocky* as Franky paraded in his new running gear. An almond pair of shoes—decorated with purple stripes and neon green soles—was dangling from his neck.

Franky and about forty other traders headed for the only track anyone could think of: an anomalous O on the Lower East Side of Manhattan in Alphabet City. The track was dark and in a seemingly dangerous neighborhood. "Within a block we could have bought enough crack for all of us," said one trader.

At the track Franky's backers—twenty-two men in gray suits—began to bicker about whether Franky should conserve his energy or run a warm-up lap. Franky ran the lap. The traders watched his stride. The odds shifted against him.

Then the race began. The traders shouted and laid yet more bets as Franky disappeared in the darkness at the far end of the track. The odds shifted toward Franky as he finished his first quarter mile strongly (in 1:48). But his second quarter mile was slower (1:52), and his third was slower still (2:00). For his supporters to win the bet, he'd have to finish the last quarter mile in under 1:50. "Our only concern," says one of Franky's backers matter-of-factly, "was that he might die before he finished and piss all our money away." But Franky didn't dare die and leave John Gutfreund $500 out of pocket. He raced home in 1:47 for the last quarter mile. His time for the mile: 7:27. He collapsed as he crossed the finish line. "I had to hand it to him," says a trader who lost $4,500 on the race, "he gutsed it out."

About the time that Franky was crawling off the track and into the grass, sucking into his blood as much oxygen as nature would allow, the modern era on Wall Street was drawing to a close in the pages of *Time*. The Street's long-running vaudeville act was suddenly playing to an audience of tomato-throwing philistines. But the shepherd's crook is nowhere in sight. The Street is not about to give back the emancipation it has won in the last ten years from the conventional rules of social behavior. The show goes on, muted only slightly by recent events. As one of the Salomon traders put it wistfully, "Wall Street's not what it used to be. If Franky had run two years ago, there'd have been $100,000 on the race."

Leveraged Rip-Off

If F. Ross Johnson, the president of RJR Nabisco, succeeds in his plan to take his company private in a $17.6 billion leveraged buyout (LBO), it will be the largest single business transaction in history. (LBO specialists Kohlberg Kravis & Roberts have made a rival bid of $20 billion.) Maybe this will finally bring leveraged buyouts—perhaps the Reagan era's most distinctive contribution to the culture of finance—the skeptical attention they deserve.*

Management-led LBOs, in which a company's managers use borrowed money to buy the company from its shareholders, have become the easiest way for people not born with $100 million to ensure that their children don't similarly suffer. America's first buyout billionaire was John Kluge of Metromedia Inc., who turned a $3 billion profit for himself in eliminating his shareholders. There have been others. And unlike, say, winnings from real estate speculation, LBO money is hoovered in with an inordinate amount of self-righteousness, probably because of what the beneficiaries hear and read about themselves. *Business Week* calls them brave risk-takers and draws little cartoons of them shooting rapids and flying hot air balloons. *Forbes* nods approvingly at their wealth. *Fortune* lists them copiously among America's 50 most interesting businesspeople. The only question usually raised is whether our heroes will win the

*This piece was written 14 November 1988.

day (they usually do). But what is really worth discussing is whether
our heroes and their deals should be outlawed.

Management-led LBOs became big business before anyone
gave them much thought. The volume of management buyouts in-
creased from 46 deals worth $4.8 billion in 1984 to 54 deals worth
$16.6 billion in 1987. The RJR Nabisco deal (involving the com-
pany formed when Nabisco, the food conglomerate, merged with
R. J. Reynolds, the tobacco purveyor, in 1985) is larger than all of
last year's deals combined.

Hold the applause for a moment. As several observers have
pointed out, the very idea of management buying out its shareholders raises a conflict of interest. How can the manager of a publicly
held company represent the interest of shareholders—which is what
they are paid to do—at the same time that they are attempting to buy
the company from the shareholders at the lowest possible price?
Doesn't that put them on both sides of the negotiating table at once?

The usual answer from seasoned LBO men starts with a sigh
and ends with a bored look: spare me the theory, buddy, we're
talking about the future of American industry here. Our newest
business heroes argue that America is in decline specifically because
the American conglomerates built in the 1960s are anachronisms
run by poor and indolent managers. To this there are only two
solutions. Either we throw the managers out and replace them with
unpopular hostile raiders and even less popular foreign companies,
or we turn the managers into entrepreneurs. "Entrepreneurs" are
never lazy or dumb. Knowing that he will go down with the ship
and also that he will benefit directly from smooth sailing, the owner-
manager skippers the newly privatized business more efficiently
than when he was merely an employee.

If it is true that privately held companies are inherently more
efficient than publicly traded ones, American capitalism—which is
dominated by large, publicly owned corporations—is based on an
enormous fallacy, and generations of business propaganda about the
wonders of widespread share ownership have been a gigantic fraud.
This may well be the case, but the advent of LBOs does not prove it.

Consider the buyout of Macy's, completed two years ago. Edward K. Finklestein, now the company's largest stockholder,
worked at Macy's for 39 years. In June 1985 Finklestein, then chair-

man, raised the idea of a buyout with Macy's board of directors, which included Beverly Sills; Robert Schwartz, the chairman of Metropolitan Life; and Lawrence Fouraker, former dean of the Harvard Business School. Outside directors are supposedly the guardians of shareholders' interests vis-à-vis management. Finklestein told board members he was losing executives to competitors because he couldn't compensate them properly. The board was skeptical. Finklestein had been given a free hand in running Macy's. He had bought himself a $15 million Gulfstream jet with shareholder's money. No one questioned his business judgment. Under his management, Macy's had prospered. But why did he need to own the company in order to pay his executives whatever it took to keep them?

Initially, the board was strongly opposed to a buyout. This upset Finklestein. He argued that his bid of $68 a share was 50 percent higher than the market price, 165 percent of the tangible book value, and 18.4 times earnings. A few weeks later the board mysteriously agreed to discuss a management buyout. The reason for their change of heart has not been formally disclosed, but in a deposition, board member Barbara Scott Preiskal said that the board was made to fear that if it didn't consider a buyout, all of Macy's management, led by Finklestein, would quit. Whatever the case, the board capitulated. But it told Finklestein that he had to "shop" the company, i.e., find the best bid for it in the market by showing it to any potential buyers.

Who knows how vigorously he pursued this task. Another LBO-hungry company chairman, described in *Inc.* magazine, relied on the red carnation approach to displaying his company. Whenever a potential buyer showed up to tour the factory floor, the chairman wore a red carnation to signal his employees to "talk the place down." Five companies requested confidential information about Macy's, and two actually met with Finklestein and Macy's president Mark Handler, but in the end no one competed with them to buy the company. Finklestein and friends were the only bidder.

Finklestein wanted to pay $68 a share, and the board of directors asked for $70. No sweat. Finklestein's financial advisers, Goldman, Sachs, claimed not to be able to finance a buyout at $70 a share, after which the Macy's board came down to Finklestein's price. The board then hired an adviser, Wolfensohn & Co., which agreed in January 1986 that $68 a share was fair.

Finklestein became an "owner-manager." The actual deal he cut for himself, however, shows how misused that phrase can be. At $68 a share, Finklestein took a $9,755,280 profit on share options he held in Macy's stock. Of that, he put back in $4,375,000. In other words, he had less of his own money riding on the future of the company after his buyout than before. In return for this relatively modest financial commitment, he got 4.9 percent of the new, private company's stock and voting rights on *all* the shares. Handler received a 2.4 percent interest, and 345 other executives divided 12 percent of the shares in exchange for a nominal investment.

In June 1986 the public shareholders met in New York to vote on the proposal. In the six weeks before the meeting, half of Macy's stock changed hands. That is typical of the frenetic trading that buyouts stimulate. Betting the deal would go through at $68, arbitrageurs bought any shares they could below that price. Institutional and individual investors, less able to assess the chance of the deal going through, sold out to them. For the arbs, the process is a self-fulfilling prophecy: Once they control a majority of the stock, the deal is certain to go through. By the time of the Macy's meeting, the votes were concentrated in hands of market players who were thinking about nothing but a quick turn on their positions.

There was never a meaningful debate on the merits of the buyout. The board of directors normally joins the chairman at the dais, but at this one Finklestein sat alone. (The board members, bless their hearts, were given seats in the front row.) One shareholder, Charles Tannenbaum, noted that Macy's had invested several hundred million dollars that, according to the company's own earnings projection, were about to pay off. But this was neglected, he felt, in the price the shareholders received. Shareholders knew that at one point the board had objected violently to a buyout at $68 a share and that a year later, with the stock market much higher, had approved one at the same price. No one would tell them why. Tannenbaum questioned Finklestein for 40 minutes, but Finklestein—on the advice of counsel—refused to answer him.

Finklestein and his associates bought the entire company for about $3 billion, virtually all of it borrowed. A year later—after the stock market crash—they offered a 40 percent interest in Macy's in lieu of cash in a bid to buy another chain of retail stores called Federated. They valued the 40 percent stake at $2.4 billion (including the taking on of about $1.4 billion in debt). That made their valuation for all of Macy's about $6 billion. Finklestein's stake, for which he paid $4.375 million, is now worth $122.5 million. Seventy other Macy's executives who participated in the buyout have become millionaires.

What magic have Finklestein and company worked to double the value of the company? Well, for a start, there are the brown bags. A McKinsey report intended as a paean to LBOs notes that Macy's said it saved a million dollars a year by standardizing its shopping bags and buying them in bulk. Some might think that buying bags in bulk is something even the most indolent corporate management might think of. How naive! Not until *after* a buyout do these little efficiencies become obvious. And guess what else. According to *Business Week,* "One California executive pared $200,000 from his division's annual budget by ending the rental of houseplants for corporate offices." And of course, "In the new Macy's, Finklestein believes, everyone from the sales clerks to the top executives deserves to be rewarded for doing a good job." Now who'd ever have thought of that?

The amazing thing about all these brilliant changes is that they are being carried out by the very same people responsible for the abuses they rectify. And it's not as if the old shareholders had insisted that each store have customized brown bags and each office have $200,000 of houseplants. If indeed these changes doubled the value of Macy's virtually overnight, it is a scandal that the beneficiaries set the stage by screwing things up in the first place.

But Macy's has enriched Finklestein et al. for different reasons. Part of the magic is in the new financial structure of the company. Like all buyouts, it has been stripped of equity and laden with debt. Shareholders have been replaced by bondholders. Before the buyout, Macy's had about ten dollars in equity for every dollar in debt. After the buyout, that ratio was reversed: one dollar in equity for every ten in debt. Because the interest on debt is deductible, Macy's will probably not pay taxes for years. As the World's Greatest Investor, Warren Buffet, has said, "If you can eliminate the government as a 46 percent partner, the business will be far more valuable." Tax arbitrage is not something that new owner-managers like to highlight. That one of America's largest retail chains pays less in taxes than Ronald Reagan's secretary undermines their message that America needs more entrepreneurs like them.

There have been a lot of inconclusive debates about whether highly indebted companies can survive a recession. Unlike dividends, which can be reduced or canceled in bad times, interest on debt must be paid or you're out of business. But it is worth pointing out that the people who created the debt do not have a whole lot of personal exposure if the whole shebang blows up. The person who introduced leverage to Macy's was Finklestein. If Macy's goes bankrupt, Finklestein becomes a temporarily unemployed multimillionaire. While old-fashioned entrepreneurs sunk with their ships, new-fangled ones build themselves life rafts filled with goodies. They are free lunch entrepreneurs: no risk, all reward.

Most of the financial exposure is transferred to the passengers—institutional investors who buy the junk bonds. Junk bonds are fast displacing equity in pension funds, savings and loans, and insurance companies. These investors sell out their equity holdings to the new robber barons and are then sold bonds by the robber barons' investment bankers. The ultimate exposure of bankruptcy lies, through a veil of intermediaries, with the small investor whose savings reside with the institutions.

The other unmentioned reason Macy's is worth so much more now than what its managers paid for it, besides the tax angle, is that Finklestein's group simply paid too little. For example, Macy's owned eight shopping malls. because American companies hold assets on their books at cost, the old Macy's listed the malls at a total value of about $100 million. Perhaps it appeared generous, therefore, when Finklestein and his associates valued the malls at $250 million in the buyout. (Recall that Finklestein boasted to the board that he was willing to pay 165 percent of book value for the company.) Three months after the buyout, Finklestein sold the malls to an Australian company for $555 million. Why didn't Finklestein get the bright idea to sell the malls six months earlier, when he was working for the public shareholders? You know why.

Despite the abuses of the system, it's not implausible that an economic system dominated by owner-managers is more efficient than one dominated by publicly owned corporations run by hired guns. If so, the old corporate form is obsolete, and the problem is how we get from here to there with the lowest "Kluge factor," an issue that is not even discussed by the market-watchers. However, if the justification for LBOs is owner management, you would think that businesses taken private would remain private. Most of the time they don't.

One of the first acts of the new owner-managers of Macy's was to register for a public offering of their stock. Finklestein has apparently ceased to be troubled as he once was about losing executives to the competition. Or maybe the executives have all become so rich that it is useless to hope that they will continue to hold daytime jobs. In any case, a public share issue or some more complicated form of sellout is expected soon. One thing you can be sure of is that when the time comes for Finklestein and company to pull the ripcord, the remaining real estate will be fully priced. Nothing undermines the argument that these buyouts are good for society so much as the sight of the new owner-managers bailing out. In 1987, according to IDD information services, there were 47 so-called reverse LBOs. Some of the companies were not private for more than six months.

There is nothing inherently uncompetitive about publicly owned corporations. Take a peek at our bogeymen. The German and the Japanese economies are based on the postwar American model of share ownership of publicly held companies, managed by just the sort of salaried dinosaurs LBO advocates want to rid our society of—low salaries, too, by American standards.

In a series of articles in *Barron's*, journalist Ben Stein has argued persuasively that the entire LBO game is a racket. He likes to harp on the role played by investment bankers, paid by management ostensibly on behalf of the shareholders, who systematically render lowball estimates of the value of companies in management buyouts. Investment banker middlemen do very well. In Macy's, for example, Goldman Sachs got $31.25 million plus a 2 percent equity stake, now worth $50 million. But investment bankers aren't explicitly assigned the task of caring for shareholders. Management is. And with heroes like these, American business doesn't need villains.

Ski Lift Tiff

On October 25, 1988 Henry Kravis, partner of the Wall Street leveraged buyout firm Kohlberg Kravis Roberts (KKR), made his bid to become a footnote in history. He offered to pay $90 a share, or $20 billion, for RJR Nabisco, purveyor of Fig Newtons, Del Monte green beans, and Winston cigarettes. That set a record for the largest bid ever made for a public company. The old record bid had been made the previous day, also for RJR Nabisco, by a team consisting of Nabisco's management and Wall Street investment bankers Shearson Lehman.

Peter Cohen, the CEO of Shearson Lehman, was heartbroken when he heard about Kravis's rival bid. "We ski together and socialize together," said Cohen, "and I thought there was a higher level of conduct called for here." Imagine, just when you think you can trust a competitor, he goes and competes against you. Distinctly ungentlemanly, wouldn't you say? Before you know it, Pete, Hank'll be cutting in lift lines.

After KKR's bid, Cohen, understandably, decided he had better have a word with his former friend Kravis. "I can't believe you are interfering in my deal," said Cohen to Kravis.

"I must be in this deal," said Kravis to Cohen, "I can't afford not to. It's my franchise."

What is more, Kravis blames Cohen for violating their little understanding. "They [Shearson Lehman] learned the business from us. Now they're turning around trying to elbow us out of our business," said an employee of KKR.

Now boys, think about what you are saying. It's one thing for investment bankers to turn corporate America into a board game. It's quite another for them to divide up the properties in advance. Cohen and Kravis are being less than discreet about the new, widespread desire on Wall Street (now that investment banks have gotten into the business of buying companies for themselves, instead of just representing them) to keep the prices down. Had Kravis not interfered, Cohen might have snapped up Nabisco for a song.

There's another word for what this tiff is about: collusion. Their indignant cries of foul sound strangely like the feuding between Arab oil ministers when an OPEC member exceeds its quotas. True, OPEC is a seller's cartel, and Kravis and Cohen are buyers. But there is nothing different about the principles underpinning a buyer's cartel. There aren't many buyers of $20 billion companies (perhaps as few as two), just as there aren't many sellers of crude oil. If they get together, they can set their purchase price to maximize their profits as would a rational monopolist. And as long as you can be confident no one can top your bid, you don't have to offer as much.

What is surprising is how openly Cohen and Kravis are beefing about the cartel busting up. It is a tribute to how little respect they have for those who might interfere with their game and to how much money they stand to make. The stakes must be high for the boardrooms to be leaking as freely as they are. So before getting too wrapped up in the tragedy of a broken friendship, the shards of which they have trodden upon each day recently* in the pages of the *Wall Street Journal*, let's have a look at what the Nabisco deal means for these two men.

In September the CEO of RJR Nabisco, F. Ross Johnson, decided to buy out his shareholders. He wanted, like so many managers these days, to own his own company. To get it, reports Bryan Burrough of the *Journal*, "Mr. Johnson turned to *his* close friend, James Robinson, chairman of American Express Co., Shearson's parent, about backing a buyout." The buyout will be accomplished in the manner of all leveraged buyouts (LBOs). The Big Fig and other assets of RJR Nabisco will be pledged as collateral, much as

*November 1988

one pledges one's house to obtain a mortgage. The only thing unusual about the proposed deal is its size. Size is important. If Nabisco can be mortgaged, so can other giants. The first man to do a giant deal becomes the world's expert in giant deals. The winner of the Nabisco auction will stand first in line for the others. The current market value of General Motors, for example, is a mere $24 billion. Sears, Mobil, Eastman Kodak also become fair game once Nabisco has been bought.

To buy Nabisco, Johnson and friends needed to borrow as much as $17 billion from banks and institutional investors in the form of junk bonds. After the stock market crash, it would have been harder to borrow $17 billion against a company's assets. A few institutional investors changed their ways for good after the crash, feeling in their bones that the crash demonstrated that company values are subject to wild and unpredictable swings.

But to everyone else the crash in October 1987 had no real lasting meaning. The stock market dropped. Then it stopped dropping. That's all. It was just after the crash, the *Journal* reports, that Kravis, over dinner, first raised the idea of a buyout with Johnson. He knew he'd have no trouble finding lenders for the deal. The goal was clear: to buy the company from the shareholders for less than it was worth, auction it in pieces at fair market values, and pocket the difference.

However, there's more than one way to skin a shareholder, and Kravis and Johnson fell out over technique. RJR Nabisco breaks down, roughly, into two parts: food and tobacco. Kravis wanted to keep the food and sell the cigarettes. Johnson wanted to keep the cigarettes and sell the food. Kravis, the trader, was thinking like a businessman. He saw that, although the tobacco business was extremely profitable, its future was jeopardized by growing public awareness of the hazards of smoking.

Johnson, the businessman, was thinking like a trader. He saw that the prices of food companies were temporarily inflated by mergers and acquisitions activity (mainly by other tobacco companies trying frantically to diversify). He also saw that tobacco companies were undervalued by the stock market, as investors ran from the surgeon general. A Wall Street equity trader would applaud Johnson's instincts. It isn't surprising that he possesses these. Johnson was, in the late 1950s in Canada, an equity trader himself.

The superiority of his trading skills is not the explanation John-son gives for neglecting Kravis's overtures. According to the *Journal*, Johnson thinks Kravis is a "stripper," or a person who buys a company with the aim of selling it off in pieces. That stripping is precisely what he and Shearson plan to do once they own Nabisco seems not to have tempered Johnson's views.

With the stock market recovering and junk bond buyers again hot to trot, the Nabisco deal has a certain inevitability about it, especially in view of what its creators stand to gain. Shearson and Johnson's bid of $75 a share was thought ridiculously low by others on Wall Street; so low, in fact, that the shares immediately traded up to $77 in anticipation of a higher bid. One Wall Street analyst told me he thought the fair price was $105 a share. If true, there is more than $6 billion of fat in the deal for Shearson and Johnson.

Shareholders, in the end, are going to get less than they deserve. But how much less? If there is any justice in the world, Nabisco should be sold to the highest stripper. If Kravis will pay $15 a share more than Cohen and Johnson, he should have the company. But Cohen is hurt that Kravis would fulfill the promise of capitalism in this way.

No doubt Cohen and Kravis will try to work out their differ-ences. If the two cooperate, it is unlikely some hitherto unan-nounced third party will spoil the fun. Most, if not all, of the finan-cial institutions able and willing to raise $17 billion for a risky venture are already committed to one side or the other. Morgan Stanley, Merrill Lynch, Drexel Burnham, and Wasserstein Perella are working for Kravis. American Express (of course) and a Japa-nese insurance company are working for Cohen. Kravis has offered Cohen a $125 million fee to "join forces" with him. Cohen's initial response was no—$125 million is far less than Cohen stands to gain without Kravis. But Cohen has told Kravis he'd value him as a 50-50 partner. If Kravis can dig down a little more deeply, who knows, perhaps he can salvage a rewarding friendship.

Barbarians
at the Trough

I'm a goddamn partner! I'm a goddamn partner! Now let me in!" The takeover lawyer stood outside a conference room in the New York offices of Skadden, Arps—*his* goddamn firm! It was the climax of the battle for RJR Nabisco, and sealed bids for the company were arriving from Kohlberg Kravis Roberts, First Boston, and Shearson. A security guard had been told to let in bids but not people. So the lawyer began to scream. Like all of Wall Street, he wanted in. Like all of Wall Street, he seemed to believe that everything important in life was at stake.

This sort of embarrassing behavior crops up on nearly every page of Bryan Burrough and John Helyar's *Barbarians at the Gate: The fall of RJR Nabisco.* There was, for example, a nasty catfight between Henry Kravis and Peter Cohen, the CEO of Shearson Lehman, that included Cohen's memorable words upon hearing that Kravis intended to bid against him: "We ski together and we socialize together, and I thought there was a higher level of conduct called for here." Kravis's reported comment was that he had a "franchise" to protect.

The exchange sounded trivial in the wake of the audacious bid for RJR Nabisco by its CEO, F. Ross Johnson. Johnson, you may recall, offered $75 a share for a company that some analysts (including Johnson's own staff) valued as high as $111 a share. He and his adviser, Shearson, appeared to be creaming off billions at the expense of shareholders. No doubt the image of the deal that lingers in the public mind is the bemused face of Johnson on the cover of *Time* magazine, above the caption: "A Game of Greed." But to finger Ross Johnson alone and mere greed as his motive is, to my mind, too simple, too pat, too *easy*. Many reputations were sullied in the buyout of RJR Nabisco, which was not a game of greed only but also of ego, vanity, and fear.

Bryan Burrough (who quoted Cohen in the *Wall Street Journal*) and John Helyar obviously sensed that there was far more to the story than the public had been told. They went after it. Henry Kravis, Peter Cohen, Jim Robinson, Theodore Forstmann, Bruce Wasserstein, and assorted minions all spilled their versions of events into the reporters' notebooks. The resulting 544-page book is among the longest-ever accounts of a single business deal. It may also be the best. The fates of big companies subject to takeover bids are now determined by a Byzantine web of alliances on Wall Street. ("You have to understand these people," says a Kravis aide. "They all want to be friends with each other.") We now have something like a blueprint of the web.

In their sketches of Wall Street's leading deal makers, Burrough and Helyar return time and again not to greed but to fear: the sheer terror evoked by the mere thought of being excluded from the biggest deal in history. There is a remarkable scene in which a vengeful Henry Kravis accuses his Drexel adviser, Jeff "Mad Dog" Beck, of leaking word of Kravis's bid to the *New York Times* and the *Journal* (as Burrough would have been on the receiving end of the leak, he must particularly relish the story):

" 'I can't believe you did this to me,' Kravis seethed.

"Beck immediately grew panicky. 'I didn't do it. Henry, you gotta believe me. I didn't do it!'

" 'These articles sure lead me to believe you did. . . . That's it, Jeff. I don't want you at any more meetings.'

"Beck became hysterical. . . . 'Henry, it wasn't me,' he said. 'I didn't do it! I didn't do it! You gotta believe me! It was Wasserstein! It had to be Wasserstein!' "

You half expect to hear Beck's screams as his kneecaps are blown off by KKR henchmen.

Wall Street's attorneys seem hardly more graceful under pressure than Wall Street's investment bankers. In a wonderfully comic scene, four of them crowd into a taxi and race from Wall Street to midtown Manhattan. They carry the all-important Shearson-Johnson bid for RJR Nabisco. Minutes before the bid is due, their cab becomes wedged in traffic two blocks from the drop site. One of the lawyers in the taxi, called Truesdell, takes nervous calls on his portable telephone every five minutes from Johnson's counsel—a man named Goldstone. When it grows clear that Truesdell may be a few minutes late, Goldstone panics:

" 'Get out of the cab and run!' he barked at Truesdell. The four attorneys piled from the taxi and began sprinting the two long blocks to Skadden, Arps. By then Johnson [who observed the scene with complete detachment, as if it didn't concern him in the least] was laughing uncontrollably. 'I hope your guy was a cross-country runner,' he told Goldstone, 'because there's no way he's going to make it. . . .' "

From here it reads like an action scene from *Revenge of the Nerds:*

"Goldstone's eyes were glued to the clock. They weren't going to make it." So while the lawyers are still sprinting, he faxes the bid in. While the fax is feeding into Skadden, Arps, Goldstone "listened to Truesdell's labored breathing over the portable phone.

" 'We're at 55th and Second!' "

And so on until the four lawyers in a scrum plunge into the lobby of Skadden, Arps. They head toward an elevator . . . when out of their phone they hear: "Wait! Wait! Wait!" The dividend rate on the preferred stock has to be recalculated.

With the possible exceptions of Teddy Forstmann and Henry Kravis (who loathe each other), no Wall Street person gives the impression he could survive without the copious fees from the deal. Many appear to have counted their winnings before the deal even began. In one early meeting Bruce Wasserstein and Morgan Stanley's Eric Gleacher pull long faces, as if they were "little boys asking for a raise in their allowances," and tell Kravis they want him to pay them each $50 million for their services. We grow curious, as the deal proceeds, about the basis for their demands. For not only does Kravis neglect their advice, he also excludes them from key discussions for fear that they'll leak secrets to the press. At one point, as the deal is being cinched, Kravis tells an aide, "Get all the bankers into a conference room and stay with 'em. And don't let any of them use the phones, especially Wasserstein." Kravis, it turns out, bought Wasserstein not for his advice, but rather to prevent him from beating the bushes for competing bidders. Fifty million dollars to put Bruce on ice!

At about the same time in the enemy camp, Peter Cohen and John Gutfreund of Salomon Brothers sit with an incredulous Teddy Forstmann and tally a list of fees that runs for pages. "Forstmann," the authors write, "thought the list would go on forever. He asked questions but only pretended to write down the answers. It was surreal." At last the end arrives. They decide the package could amount to $1.9 billion. But wait! Forstmann's brother notices that all the numbers are based on a miscalculation of the offer for RJR Nabisco. It turns out no one in the room knows exactly how much money they need to borrow to buy the company. Still, they know their fees to the last decimal place. Putting RJR Nabisco on the Wall Street auction block, Forstmann reflects, was "like throwing a hundred pounds of bloody meat into a shark pool."

Strangely, the man who brought the meat to the shark party appears the most willing to sacrifice his portion. Once Ross Johnson puts his company into play by announcing his intention to buy it from his shareholders, he seems content to sit back and watch these silly Wall Street people debase themselves. He clowns around about the three rules of Wall Street: "Never play by the rules, never pay in cash, and never tell the truth." He never ceases to be amused by what investment bankers will think of next. When his bankers, Shearson and Salomon, explain that they intend to pay for the company in part with PIK (pay-in-kind) bonds, which pay interest not in cash but in more bonds, Johnson jokes, "Hey, why don't we start a new company, and it'll be all PIK. . . . I mean, we have found something that's better than the U.S. printing press. And they've got it all down here on Wall Street. . . . You could solve the Third World debt crisis with this stuff. It's a brand-new currency. . . ."

He then doubles up with laughter and starts to mimic a printing press. "Chuck-oon, chuck-oon, chuck-oon," he says. "Just print it and let her fly."

Johnson is by far the most likable character in the book. Unlike the Wall Street lot, he doesn't appear to have a petty or venomous bone in his body. He is a swaggering rogue: ribald, mischievous, careless, and unprincipled—Sir John Falstaff in a suit. He has several corporate jets, twenty-four country club memberships, and a multi-million-dollar collection of celebrity jocks called Team Nabisco, all paid for by the long-suffering shareholders of RJR Nabisco. (Johnson mocks the idea that shareholders have any say in how RJR Nabisco is run. He refers to his board of directors as "pseudo-independent" and keeps them happy with a steady flow of perks.) When he isn't playing golf with Jack Nicklaus, Johnson is pounding brews with Dandy Don Meredith. The authors attribute his decision to put his company in play to boredom, and the more we read of the man, the truer this rings.

Still, it is in their assessment of Johnson that the authors' case begins to creak. Johnson is made to undergo a dramatic (and implausible) character transformation midway through the book. From a shrewd manipulator who always gets his way he becomes the pawn of Peter Cohen and John Gutfreund—incapable as they seem throughout of manipulating anything to their advantage. He sounds bewildered when told how much money he'd need to buy his company: "Seventeen billion dollars. Fuck, I'll be going around on my hands and knees like a monkey with an organ grinder to find $17 billion." He is cast as the chief victim when Henry Kravis steps into the ring: "Johnson was lulled by the same fundamental fallacy embraced by the Shearson executives," the authors write. "For all the talk of possible competitors, most of them were convinced their bid, if launched, would be unopposed. They felt certain that no one, not even Kravis, would attempt a buyout this size without the help of a management team to identify the best ways to cut costs."

To the extent that there is an editorial line in the book (and it is pedaled softly), it is this: thieves from Wall Street were picking the pockets of rubes from the South, while the rubes from the South were trying to pick the pockets of their shareholders. A much more plausible explanation for Johnson's seeming blindness to the risk of losing his job was that he was genuinely indifferent to the prospect. "You don't understand," he tells a colleague at one point. "We don't have to win at all. . . . It's poker. You can't put your pride in front of your mind." Bored with the status quo, Johnson engineered a new and exciting no-lose game for himself. If he won, he became rich. If he lost, he also became rich, thanks to the golden parachutes his board had approved.

In a telling moment near the end (an account Johnson denies), when the special committee of RJR Nabisco directors is preparing to hand the company over to Henry Kravis, Johnson telephones his old buddy, the chairman of the committee, Charles Hugel. Hugel is sure Johnson is calling to plead for the company. But the first thing out of Johnson's mouth has nothing to do with the committee's decision. "We've heard they are going to cancel the golden parachutes," he says. "Is that true?" That isn't the voice of a man clinging to his job.

The board of course left Johnson's golden parachute intact. And the reader is left to wonder if Ross Johnson, as he descended gently to earth, had any regrets. After all, stockholders, bondholders, customers, and workers were all trod upon. Before the bid was announced, employees in the Atlanta headquarters of RJR Nabisco, worried about the security of their jobs, apparently consulted psychics.

Please tell us what the future holds.

" 'I don't see this as a job for the rest of your life,' the psychic said.

" 'What do you see?'

"The psychic closed her eyes and appeared to concentrate for a long moment. Then she said, 'It just kind of goes . . . poof.' "

The Mystery of
the Disappearing
Employees

"Sunlight is the best of all disinfectants."
—*Bruce Wasserstein to Henry Kravis*
on the eve of the battle for RJR Nabisco.

The switchboard operator at RJR Nabisco put our call through to an irritable woman in the personnel department. My colleague and I were looking for a division of RJR Nabisco called RJR Nabisco Broadcast. Did she know where we might find it? "It was dispatched and is no longer with us," she said irritably. I liked that—Dispatched. It made it sound as though the unit had been sent away on a long and delicate mission. Could she tell me what had become of the victims? "No." So we let it drop.

Anyway, we were not being entirely forthcoming ourselves. On October 16, 1989, there had been a few paragraphs in the second section of the *Wall Street Journal* announcing the termination of a division of RJR Nabisco called RJR Nabisco Broadcast, which had purchased television time for RJR Nabisco commercials. It was a plain, boring, gray little piece—except for one thing. RJR Nabisco Broadcast had been moved from Atlanta to New Jersey in September, only weeks before it was . . . un . . . dispatched—end of story. But surely this was very strange. Why would any company—and especially a company under the infallible Henry Kravis—put its people through the trauma of moving their lives some eight hundred chilly miles north, only to fire them a few weeks later?

RJR Nabisco has come to stand as a symbol for the entire lever-aged buyout business. Yet because it is now private, very little of the hard data emerges from the shop floor. The justification for its leveraged buyout was that, like all LBOs, it would put control of the company into more efficient hands. Now more than a year after the deal was done, no one except Henry Kravis has any idea whether this is in fact what happened. And he's not telling. Therein lay the intrigue of the tiny gray announcement in the *Wall Street Journal.* It looked like evidence for what no one would ever care to admit: that a great deal of bullshit goes on inside a company after its leveraged buyout, just as it did before.

The search for survivors of RJR Nabisco Broadcast began fruitlessly with the irritable woman in personnel at RJR Nabisco. Another RJR spokeswoman would say only that they had been "eliminated." (Note to public relations people: the cold-blooded verbs—eliminate, dispatch—sound far more sinister than the red-blooded alternatives—fired, axed, body-slammed.) There had been fourteen people in the purged unit; that's all she could say. A dozen phone calls yielded not a shred of evidence as to the current whereabouts of these fourteen people. And after a week I began to doubt whether they had ever lived. Agatha Christie couldn't have arranged for characters to disappear more effectively. A group of highly visible people who only three months before had worked for one of the largest corporations in the United States had vanished as if down a crack. What I didn't know was that they had been paid by RJR Nabisco to do just this. But I run ahead of the story.

Having been turned away by RJR Nabisco itself, I called the outplacement firm that handles the massive and growing business from RJR Nabisco—Right Associates. They claimed not to have the slightest idea where the Broadcast people were—even though, in theory, they had put them there. The next obvious place to try was the television networks; RJR Nabisco Broadcast had been responsible for buying $250 million of network and cable airtime. ABC and CBS said they'd think about it and call back. They did and they didn't. Then at NBC there appeared to be a breakthrough, where a helpful-sounding woman answered the phone.

"I'm looking for the person who dealt with RJR Nabisco Broadcast before it was dispatched."

"Oh," she said, "you want to talk to Gary Wold, and he's right here."

Blessed woman! She was going to give me Gary Wold, and

Gary Wold was going to solve the mystery. Gary Wold was right there. But . . . he was sure taking his time. When at last a voice came on the line, it was not Gary Wold's.

"I'm sorry," said the woman, "but Gary Wold's not in."

I see. Perhaps, I thought, the unit had committed mass seppuku in New Jersey. Having been discredited in the eyes of their peers, they decided to end it all right then and there. I checked the obituaries of the past few months in the *New York Times*—no luck. Perhaps, I thought, they'd run away from home. I checked the sides of milk cartons in Gristedes—no luck. They don't put pictures on them anymore. Perhaps, I thought, they are socially prominent New Yorkers who have since married. I checked the wedding announcements in the *Times*. And there I found my lead to a human being we shall call Deep Despair, still so frightened by its former employer that it refused to be identified, even by sex.

In 1986 RJR Nabisco Broadcast was based in New York, headed by John Martin, a close friend of the former CEO of RJR Nabisco, Ross Johnson. It then moved from New York to Atlanta in 1987. In late 1988 Ross Johnson lost the battle to buy his own company, and Henry Kravis took over. This was bad news for RJR Nabisco Broadcast, as it was closely identified with Johnson. Not surprisingly, the new management targeted Broadcast for removal. That spring a team from McKinsey was sent in to "blow holes in the organization," according to one close to the situation. Instead McKinsey found that the unit was well run and saved the company something like $4 million a year by concentrating the media-buying power under one roof.

Nevertheless the employees of RJR Nabisco Broadcast found they had a new boss. They reported to John Greeniaus, the CEO of Nabisco. And on September 18, 1989, Greeniaus moved the group from Atlanta to New Jersey. Moving to New Jersey isn't a universally appealing prospect, and many RJR Nabisco Broadcast employees simply refused to go. Peter Chrisanthopoulos, the president of RJR Nabisco Broadcast, went to work coaxing his people north. He had no idea what was about to happen.

Two days into the fourth week in New Jersey, the fourteen Broadcast employees were invited into a conference room and fired. The speech they were given didn't begin to address the obvious

question: why did you move us up from Atlanta if you were going
to fire us all along? The company had even helped them to sell their
homes in Atlanta. "Everyone was still living in hotels," says Deep
Despair. "You couldn't even go home to your home because you
had no home. So everyone went back to their little hotel rooms and
said, 'So what do I do with my life now?' You were all alone."

What is more, Chrisanthopoulos had *hired* several people from
other companies during the three weeks his division spent in New
Jersey. Those people found they had quit their old jobs only to be
fired from their new ones. "We were blindsided, to say the least, and
that's probably an understatement," says Deep Despair. A black
humor gripped the department. With few exceptions, they were
badly shaken. An unfunny joke passed among them, from Hilton to
Hyatt to Marriott: what's homeless and unemployed? RJR Nabisco
Broadcast. Three months later most were still unemployed. "We're
all still looking for jobs," Deep Despair said. (Which explains why
the outplacement firm was clueless; as yet no one has been out-
placed.)

There was some consolation. RJR Nabisco makes psychiatric
care available to its employees. "They said we could keep the ther-
apy," says Deep Despair. But they weren't given an adequate explanation for their release. Instead they were handed long-tailed sever-
ance packages contingent upon keeping mum. The documents they
signed said in effect that the stream of payments from the company
to them would dry up if they talked to the press. No wonder they
disappeared.

A division was fired for no obvious commercial reason; indeed
all the evidence—former RJR Nabisco executives, the McKinsey
study, the move just three weeks before from Atlanta—suggests that
RJR Nabisco Broadcast was worth keeping. Of course this is just the
sort of careless and seemingly irrational management that a leveraged buyout is meant to root out. In truth, the idiocy of the handling
of RJR Nabisco Broadcast was *caused* by the LBO. For Broadcast
was a victim of nothing more commercial than office politics. And
the politics were a direct result of divisiveness sown into the company during the battle between Ross Johnson and Henry Kravis.
But to see this requires a bit of background.

John Greeniaus—who decided the fate of RJR Nabisco Broadcast—plays a shadowy role in the best-selling account of the buyout of RJR Nabisco, *Barbarians at the Gate*. Like Banquo's ghost, he speaks rarely but to great effect. The first we see of him, he is being told the news of the biggest business deal in history by Ross Johnson.

"Johnny, I'm going to do a leveraged buyout!"

Greeniaus was shattered. He'd been left out of the plans, because the plans stipulated that Nabisco be sold to pay off the debt after the completion of the LBO. Other men might have been elated. Greeniaus would receive more than $7 million in severance benefits and another $5 million or so in profits on RJR Nabisco stock.

"Johnny," said Johnson, "I'm going to make you rich."

But Greeniaus's first thought wasn't money. His first thought, according to this account, was, "He's blowing up Nabisco. I'm out of a job. My people are screwed." Greeniaus was also screwed. He had planned to succeed Johnson in 1990 as CEO of RJR Nabisco. Johnson had promised him the job. Now all he would get was money.

Greeniaus, in short, was the sort of man whose identity was wrapped up in a package with the company he worked for. He believed that a company was responsible for its employees, and he can no doubt keenly appreciate how traumatic it is to be dispatched by a company with which you had intended to spend the rest of your career.

Throughout the battle for RJR Nabisco, Greeniaus's humor was black. He circulated cartoons. In one an executive said, "Gentlemen, I have disquieting news. Our parent company has disowned us." Beneath this Greeniaus wrote, "So how does it feel to be orphans?"

So badly did Greeniaus wish to keep his job that he decided to foil Ross Johnson's plans. According to the book, he mailed a secret note to the RJR board saying he would help anyone who came in to bid against Johnson. As he told his right-hand man and confidant, Larry Kleinberg, CEO of Nabisco, "This is a survival game. Let's play it to the best of our ability." He knew that Henry Kravis could only outbid Johnson if someone on the inside supplied him with information. Without inside help Kravis would be forced to bid blind. Greeniaus supplied the information. He persuaded Kravis that there was enough waste at RJR Nabisco to justify a much higher price than Johnson was offering. It is not too much to say that without Greeniaus, Kravis could not have won.

But he did, which left Greeniaus in power. And Greeniaus's principled concern for the employees of Nabisco apparently did not extend to the rest of Johnson's former empire. For it was Greeniaus who issued the orders to fire RJR Nabisco Broadcast. Why he moved them to New Jersey from Atlanta three weeks before dropping the ax remains a mystery. (Greeniaus declined to comment.) According to Deep Despair, the company did not even plead a need to cut costs. "They just said something about a need to focus less on media and more on manufacturing," or whatever. How can anyone but a fool stay loyal to a company stalked by Wall Street?

We still hear a lot about the efficiencies of leveraged buyouts but almost nothing about their bitter aftertaste, which leads the winners to take their revenge on the losers, and the bonds between employee and employer forged under one CEO to be ignored by his successor. Perhaps we should hear more. But secrecy is far easier to maintain in a private company than in a public one. "I'm not going to say any more," said Deep Despair. "They could really hurt me if they find out I've spoken to you." There was a crackling in the phone line. "Yeah," said Deep Despair, "it's probably RJR Nabisco listening in."

Mr. Wall Street Goes to Washington

The most dramatic parallel between the roaring twenties and the roaring eighties is Wall Street's willingness to believe that the rest of our republic is stupid. Last month* Salomon Brothers found itself censured by the Securities and Exchange Commission for making illegal short sales during the crash of October 1987. What was interesting about the case wasn't that Salomon in the heat of the moment broke the law, but that management after sober reflection tried to hide the evidence. It initially refused to permit the SEC to inspect Salomon's books. That small act of defiance was truly haunting.

Remember Ferdinand Pecora? In the U.S. Senate investigation of Wall Street that followed the crash of 1929, it was legal counsel Pecora who grilled the witnesses. Wall Street's leaders approached those hearings in a Salomonesque spirit of obstruction, hiding behind a veneer of pompous respectability. Pecora finally resorted to a vicious smear campaign to pry off Wall Street's mask. He unearthed the tax returns of J. P. Morgan to show that the financier hadn't paid taxes in years. (This was irrelevant, of course, but it also excited public outrage.) He humiliated Richard Whitney, the president of the New York Stock Exchange, forcing him to admit to the existence on Wall Street of "pools" that manipulated stock prices. Pecora later wrote that in shaping the laws that now govern Wall

*This piece was written in July 1989.

Street—laws that gave birth to the SEC—"virtually no aid or cooperation came from the denizens of that great marketplace we euphemistically call Wall Street. Indeed they were passed in the face of the bitter and powerfully organized opposition of the financial community. That opposition was overcome principally because public indignation had been deeply aroused by the conclusive evidence of wrongdoing."

Now, as then, outdated rules govern the world of money. Now, as then, Wall Street sees the primitive brakes on its souped-up machine more as an opportunity to exploit than as a problem to correct. Now, as then, the real scandal is not that laws are occasionally broken on Wall Street but that the public interest is legally trodden upon by people who know perfectly well what they are doing might jeopardize our future welfare. That's why they dissemble.

For several reasons, I think, another attack on Wall Street's sovereignty is imminent.* First, the courts are beginning to catch up with the relatively new conflicts of interest inherent in investment banking. Takeover adviser Bruce Wasserstein, for instance, was recently castigated by the Delaware Supreme Court for having perpetrated a "fraud upon the board" of Macmillan Inc. when British press lord Robert Maxwell and the leveraged buyout firm of Kohlberg Kravis Roberts & Co. were vying for the publishing company. According to the court, Wasserstein, who had been engaged to advise Macmillan, was also giving advice to KKR. "The courts are suspicious and will no longer accept blindly the advice of bankers," said William T. Allen of the Delaware Chancery Court.

Second, House leaders Jim Wright and Tony Coelho have lost their jobs partly because their hands were found deep in the pockets of money men. In a newly chastened Washington, money is less likely to have its way. And if it no longer pays to be a friend of the Street, it may pay to be an enemy. The zeitgeist, in other words, is ripe for another Ferdinand Pecora.

Third, and more to the point, while Congress scratches its head over various financial crises, Wall Street is busy obscuring rather than clarifying issues such as the S&L fiasco and the leveraging of

*I was wrong.

corporate America. A May 25, 1989, congressional hearing on leveraged buyouts focused on a strange paper recently published by KKR. The "study," which affects an objective, academic tone, happily concludes that LBOs "increase employment, increase research and development, yield higher taxes to the federal government, keep capital spending strong, and are able adequately to handle negative events such as economic downturns."

At the hearing Emil M. Sunley, an economist with the accounting firm Deloitte, Haskins & Sells, spoke for KKR. He came with a fat briefcase and struck a pose of benign condescension, but this turned quickly into malignant indignation when he was made to look foolish. The catalyst for the change was a mild-mannered Brookings Institution economist named William Long, who sat to Sunley's left. Long has coauthored a study discrediting the KKR report. Its conclusions, Long showed, hinged on creative mathematics. The numbers were forced to fit the conclusion. The best anyone could say about LBOs, Long felt, was that it was too early to tell what they might do to the economy. Studies more credible than KKR's, however, suggest that LBOs actually *reduce* employment, capital spending, R&D, et cetera.

What was special about the hearing was its tone. Each time a point was made against him the man from KKR rocked back and forth in his chair. He frantically sifted a growing chaos of paper on his table as if somewhere in the mess a rebuttal might be found. There was none. It was hard not to feel a bit sorry for him. He was like the boy in a high-school debating class assigned to argue an impossible case—say, genocide as a means of population control. When he finally objected, weakly, that "the purpose of the study was not to analyze typical leveraged buyouts but instead to tell the KKR story," he was savaged by Massachusetts congressman Edward Markey, who rightly pointed out that the KKR study is shot through with generalizations about the positive effects of LBOs on the U.S. economy. Sunley at last fell silent. "We didn't set out to bash KKR," said a committee staffer. "It just sort of ended up that way."

This wasn't a case of just one firm trying to pull the wool over the eyes of Congress. KKR was joined by Hardwick Simmons, vicechairman of Shearson Lehman and chairman of the Securities In-

dustry Association (SIA). The SIA represents more than 585 investment banks. Simmons began by saying that "Congress should follow its neutral approach," i.e., do nothing to interfere with LBOs.
He then delivered an SIA report nearly as slippery as KKR's study.
It masqueraded as "a survey of the existing academic literature" on
LBOs. For a survey, however, it was remarkably one-sided in favor
of LBOs. It omitted most of the literature, including a seminal paper
by Benjamin Bernanke, a Princeton economics professor who
makes a strong case that the leveraging of corporate America could
end in tears. The SIA paper was a survey of little except the half-
truths and veiled threats Congress is likely to hear from investment
bankers if it tries to interrupt Wall Street's newest money game.
You've probably heard some of these before. You'll certainly hear a
few of them again:

Stop LBOs and the Japanese will overwhelm America. Or, as the
SIA report contends, "LBOs have facilitated the changes in organizational structure necessary to improve U.S. competitiveness."
What this means is that LBOs are busting up the very conglomerates Wall Street helped to create in the 1960s and 1970s. The new
vogue is for what the SIA calls "owner-managers." Never mind that
there is no hard evidence that changes in structure enhance U.S.
competitiveness. Never mind that LBOs aren't the only way to
achieve the admittedly desirable result of giving managers stakes in
their businesses. Why, if the creation of "owner-managers" is the
point of LBOs, do most of them go public again a few years after the
buyout? You'd think the SIA "survey" would raise this obvious
question. It doesn't.

Stop LBOs and the stock market will crash again. Pointing to the
crash of October 1987, the SIA warns that "the securities markets
are extremely sensitive to regulatory and legislative developments,
including unofficial remarks by policymakers." At its crudest this
sounds like blackmail. While it's undoubtedly true that the takeover
game excites the stock market, it's not at all clear that discouraging
one species of takeover—LBOs—would lead to an overall market
crash. Is it not more likely that proposed laws to curb LBOs (such as
eliminating tax breaks on corporate debt) would be met by a gradual
decline in the stock market as they wound their lethargic way
through Congress? And aren't lower stock prices a small price to

pay for a more stable financial structure in America?

Debt is good; debt works. "Perhaps the greatest misconception clouding the debate on LBOs is that as a result of recent LBO activity corporate America is becoming overleveraged," says the SIA report. Also: "Efficiency gains result in part from the discipline imposed by debt service." The SIA argument is that 1) the ratio of debt to equity in America is no greater than it has been in the past, 2) American companies carry less debt than their Japanese and German counterparts, and 3) large amounts of debt force corporate managers to be thrifty. Here again, however, nettlesome outsiders have undermined Wall Street's pitch. Professor Bernanke sat, unfortunately, directly beside SIA chairman Simmons at the hearing. And he testified: "Using high leverage to improve corporate performance is much like encouraging safe driving by putting a dagger, pointed at the driver's chest, in every car's steering wheel; it may improve driving but may lead to disaster during a snowstorm."

Bernanke's own report—entitled "Is There a Corporate Debt Crisis?"—predicts that, in a recession similar to the dip of 1974, more than 10 percent of 643 large American companies he studied would go bankrupt. Debt-to-equity ratios, like most of Wall Street's evidence presented at the hearing, are misleading, because stock market values (the equity component of the ratio) are at nearly historic highs. The ratio of debt to cash flow is a better measure of a company's ability to meet its obligations. Henry Kaufman (who quit Salomon Brothers partly because that firm was doing business he disapproved of) calculates that debt servicing today comprises 26 percent of corporate America's cash flow, compared with 22 percent in 1982 and 19 percent in 1974. As Professor Bernanke concluded, "The last time we had debt in this range was in the 1920s."

Ah, memories.

How Wall Street
Took the S & Ls
for a Ride

If you really want to know how the big money has been made on Wall Street in the 1980s, it's worth spending some time in the elevators—going down. There, you are often treated to a telling farce: three fine young men not long out of Wharton or Harvard are escorting to the lobby a chubby, middle-aged man in $105 worth of blue polyester from Sears, a necktie that looks like a television on the blink, and a Sacramento High signet ring. The young men laugh at whatever the older guy says. Clearly they don't mean it. Everything about the older guy shouts "Hick from out of town!" You can just see the young men shudder as they imagine the Rotary Club mallet on his desk back home and the Lions Club certificate of appreciation on his wall.

In other words, you are left in no doubt whatsoever as to who is the customer here. Just to complete the picture, the older guy is clutching credulously to his chest a package—a two-inch-thick job bound in plastic and whose cover reads Salomon Brothers or First Boston. It also says Scenario Analysis for Risk-Controlled Arbitrage or, perhaps, CMO Equity Analysis. This is a gift from the young men, and it comes with strings attached. Since mid 1985 risk-controlled arbitrage has been a euphemism on Wall Street for big-time gambling in the mortgage-backed bond market. CMO Equity (*b.* 1987) is a particularly slippery mortgage investment. The CMO stands for collateralized mortgage obligation, but bond salesmen call it "toxic waste."

You have to figure that the older guy works for a savings and loan. S & L executives are the only men in history to have worn $105 suits while risking millions. You cringe at the thought of what the young men are about to do to him.

The latest estimate of the cost of bailing out the savings and loan industry is $166 billion* and still growing. Only two years ago that figure was $30 billion. You'd almost think the *Wall Street Journal* was making up bigger numbers as it went along, in order to keep its readers interested. But my point isn't that all large numbers related to government screwups are unreliable, as if they had been invented out of whole cloth (though that is probably true). It's that as this number gets bigger and bigger, no one is asking the obvious question: Where has all that money gone? Who's become filthy rich?

No doubt many Americans believe that most of the money has simply been squandered by crooked savings and loan executives on private air fleets, California beach houses, trips to Paris, and blueprints for branches on the moon. As the losses mount, however, the corruption theory starts to leak (it's not easy, even for a Texan, to embezzle $180 billion). The truth is that a lot of the money was lost legally by crazy gamblers—and a big chunk of that found its way into the pockets of the Wall Street bond traders and salesmen who encouraged the S & Ls to gamble like lunatics in the first place. There are $900,000 houses in Connecticut with two BMWs out back that have been paid for by their twenty-nine-year-old owners courtesy of the savings and loan crisis. And the beauty of it is that in milking the S & Ls, the twenty-nine-year-olds did nothing illegal.

How this came to pass is one of the strangest twists in the tale of the largest financial crisis in American history. Ten years ago Wall Street traders and Main Street thrifters were about as far apart as two groups of financial people could be. But by 1983, thanks to federal tax incentives, the savings and loan industry was trading bonds more frenetically—and more foolishly—than Wall Street ever did. And Wall Street—Salomon Brothers, in particular—was running trading books that looked a lot like multibillion dollar S & L portfolios.

---

*This was the estimate as of November 1989. Current estimates range from $300 billion to $1 trillion.

In short, the two industries collided with each other in what sometimes resembled a bloody game of sharks and minnows. All of a sudden some of Wall Street's biggest clients were also some of the most sensational failures in the S & L industry—the Financial Corporation of America, Centrust, and Lincoln Savings & Loan, to name just three. That this has been largely overlooked is a tribute both to the ignorance of the people who ostensibly regulate the savings and loan industry and to the ability of Wall Street to chew with its mouth shut while feeding at the public trough. If at any time during the early 1980s a senior Wall Street figure had explained to Congress what was going on, there's a reasonable chance Congress might have put a stop to the gambling. But no one did. As Dick Still, the former general counsel for the House Committee on Banking, Finance, and Urban Affairs, told me, "We didn't have any idea what they [investment bankers] were doing. They didn't want to help. There's not one guy I can call up there [on Wall Street] to get a straight answer." So the only way you'd know how Wall Street has pillaged the S & Ls is if you were inside the elevators watching.

As it happens, I was. I worked at Salomon Brothers, probably the single largest beneficiary of the legendary gullibility of savings and loan CEOs. The mortgage trading unit, created by Lewie Ranieri, was the firm's most profitable business in the first half of this decade; it generated perhaps $6 billion in revenues (the number is an educated guess). And its profits, until 1985, came mainly from its dealings with S & Ls.

I met my first mortgage trader after he had persuaded the CEO of a Texas savings and loan to sell $70 million of one mortgage bond and buy $70 million of another mortgage bond, much like what he had sold. The CEO, the trader said, was famously ignorant about mortgage-backed bonds. ("The S & L industry is one of the few in the world where the product is created by people who don't know much about it," observes one Salomon bond salesman.) So the CEO didn't notice that the price he received from the Salomon trader was too low and the price he paid was too high. Since the CEO had spent his career trying to please his customers—after all, he had to face them on the street from time to time—he couldn't imagine any other approach to business. More to the point, he didn't realize how ruthless a Wall Street trader can be. A Wall Street trader behaves as if each trade were his last. This Salomon trader made the $70 million swap and in a matter of seconds netted over $2 million—two million dollars!

Then he reflected.

That, he said, was why Salomon Brothers was the king.

"Jesus," I said.

"Jesus got nuttin' to do wit' it," he said.

Which was true: Jesus didn't work at Salomon Brothers.

Jesus didn't work at the Twin City Federal Bank in Minneapolis either, much as a casual inspection of the place suggests he might fit in with the corporate culture. Between 1982 and 1986 Twin City lived unwittingly by the maxim that it is better to give than to receive.

Back in 1980, Twin City was, as one employee put it, "in deep yogurt." Throughout the 1960s and 1970s it had been borrowing short-term money to make thirty-year loans at fixed rates of interest of anywhere between 4 and 8 percent. In October 1979 Paul Volcker made his stand against inflation, and the cost of short-term funds soon shot up to around 17.5 percent. Twin City found itself borrowing at 17.5 percent but still lending at 4 to 8 percent; in other words, it was hemorrhaging money.

With the help of a bond salesman working in the Chicago office of Salomon Brothers, Twin City devised a way to save itself. Instead of hunkering down and weathering the storm (which might well have worked), Twin City decided to grow its way out of its problems. It began to borrow a lot more money at 17.5 percent and to invest it in hopes of still higher returns. Lenders indulged Twin City because they knew that if Twin City went belly up, the U.S. government would repay its debts. But that is another story.

Between 1982 and 1986 Twin City's assets grew from $3.5 billion to $5.5 billion. This was in keeping with the rest of the savings and loan industry, which grew from $686 billion to $1.1 trillion during the same period. Of the $2 billion boom at Twin City at least $1.3 billion, claims a former employee, represented mortgage-backed securities purchased from Salomon Brothers in the package that came to be known and marketed as risk-controlled arbitrage. "Can you believe that name—risk-controlled arbitrage?" says one Salomon Brothers thrift salesman. "I laugh every time I hear it. It's like military intelligence."

The young lady at Twin City who was in charge of trading the $1.3 billion or thereabouts in bonds got a call each day from the young man at Salomon who had sold them to her. She enjoyed talking to him. Minnesota was cold and lonely. There wasn't another soul for hundreds of miles who owned $1.3 billion of bonds. Information was scarce. "It was funny," she says today, "Salomon always knew what was going on in Washington. I got a lot of information on changes in savings and loan regulations from them that I got from no other source." It wasn't that funny. Lewie Ranieri lobbied heavily in Washington for reforms that would enable earthbound S & Ls to spread their wings and fly.

Some days the Salomon salesman persuaded her to trade—in other words, to sell some of her bonds and buy others. She almost always followed his advice. She might trade $70 million worth, if she was feeling up to it—or more. On one day in the middle of 1985 it seems she traded $1.3 billion of mortgage bonds. She sold $650 million to Salomon, and she bought another $650 million of what amounted to pretty much the same thing. In so doing she became one of the world's biggest bond traders. (Still, this hardly compared with the roughly $17 billion portfolio of mortgage-backed securities the Financial Corporation of America was holding.) Did the young woman at Twin City know what she was about?

Well, she says, she knew that Salomon Brothers could be dangerous. "My boss had his eyes ripped on a couple of trades. Thank God they were small." But she regarded herself as savvy. She knew the value of bonds, she says, and she liked dealing with her Salomon Brothers salesman.

In 1985 Twin City acquired a new CEO, a former commercial banker named William Cooper. He wasn't like most thrift CEOs. He wore suspenders. And he waxed cynically eloquent on the subject of investment bankers. "They'll sell you shit in a heartbeat," he warned. "And they have had a party at the expense of the 3–6–3 crowd," as the savings and loan CEOs are commonly known, because of their custom of borrowing at 3 percent, lending at 6 percent, and making it to the golf course by 3 every afternoon. But he can be forgiven. One of the first things Cooper discovered upon his arrival was that his risk-controlled arbitrage package from Salomon Brothers was losing millions of dollars. As one employee of Twin

City puts it, "It turned out that it wasn't so risk-controlled, and it wasn't such an arbitrage. Everyone wondered what was going on."

In the middle of 1986, a year before Lewie Ranieri lost his job at Salomon, the young lady who put Twin City on the Wall Street map left hers. She says it was by "mutual agreement." "We've had several people who've lost their jobs because Wall Street deceived us," says one Twin City executive. The Salomon Brothers bond salesman, by way of contrast, is regarded as the star of the Chicago office; it is said he has generated more profits for Salomon than any other salesman outside of New York.

Again it was all legal, even moral, in the minds of some people on Wall Street. Twin City (now TCF Bank Savings) was a putatively sophisticated institution. Its traders should have been able to take care of themselves. That they couldn't was no one's fault but their own. It is chilling to consider that they probably did know more about what they were doing than many of Wall Street's savings and loan clients. And it lends a certain irony to the current activities of Lewie Ranieri and several other former Wall Street traders. Ranieri has bought a thrift and a mortgage company.

When Bad Things Happen to Rich People

Until recently, a case could be made that the investment bank of the 1980s had created a new species of American office worker who, at no great risk to himself and with no special skill or preparation, got very rich, very young. It's a tempting thought. And many shared it. One-third of the graduates of the Harvard Business School this decade have become investment bankers, up from 12 percent in the seventies. Outside the jammed offices of Ivy League career services, lines form in the snow of students willing to freeze just to meet somebody from Goldman Sachs.

If you were one of last year's lucky winners, you would be sitting in a training program at Salomon Brothers, First Boston, or Goldman Sachs, wondering if you still had a job. You know, because your employers have reminded you, that Wall Street is awash in warm bodies that can replace you if you ever became a drain on profits. And you have heard about the horror show that recently* played to a full, trembling house in the London office of Salomon Brothers.

It was on a Friday morning. One in five Salomon bankers was about to be canned. Management had not told them so directly, but had leaked it to the press. Salomon Brothers' staff read about its collective career prospects in the *Wall Street Journal*, section two, page one. No one knew exactly who was going to bite the dust.

*This piece was written in November 1987.

Hundreds of investment bankers sat twitching, literally in the dark, since a hurricane the previous night had blown out the lights in central London.

When the cut finally came, it was swift, cruel, and hypocritical. Being sacked did not reflect badly on one's professional ability, sackees were told. It was just something that had to be done, like an appendectomy. As the appendix left the operating room, either stunned or in tears, he was met by a waiting security guard who told him in effect that he was trespassing. He was to hand over his security pass and leave.

It was an indignity for which the Harvard Business School had left one ill-prepared, though when an investment banker is fired it is understood he is to clear out immediately—no loitering around to say goodbye, no reminiscing about old hostile takeovers, no misty-eyed reflections on that big sale of IBM bonds. There may be golden handshakes, but there are no gold wristwatches. This is just as well. The presence of the fired is as awkward in a hyperachieving investment bank as the presence of the runners-up after the Miss America contest.

Meanwhile, on the other side of town, Chemical Bank was using a finer blade to cut 18 percent of its staff. Young traders spending a day with clients at a go-cart track called in to see whether bond prices were up and learned instead that they no longer had jobs. Chemical's commercial-bank management was unprepared for the effect on investment banking egos. One fired Chemical banker was told by the personnel department on his way out the door that the company Porsche should be returned soon. The next morning he drove the Porsche onto the sidewalk in front of the bank and parked it flush against the front door. He then turned on the car alarm, locked the door, and threw the key into the Thames.

While the Porsche keys sank into the river silt in London, entire trading departments were booted out onto the street in New York, illustrating that the market for financial people is as global as the financial markets themselves. Salomon, along with its London cuts, fired its New York money-market and municipal finance departments. A wide swath of Salomon's normally loud New York trading floor is still eerily silent. Inspirational signs still hang over empty money-market seats: "Eat Stress For Breakfast," reads one.

Pictures of girlfriends and private messages remain taped to the trading positions. Scribbled over the empty seat of a redundant female trader is her view that "Men who call women sweetheart, baby, or honey should have their tiny little peckers cut off."

If it is dangerous, as John Kenneth Galbraith has argued, for these people to be at large, watch out. Shearson Lehman and L. F. Rothschild have already fired people, and Goldman Sachs, which is, as ever, private about its problems is said to be undergoing a global review of its business, with an eye to chopping off weak limbs. Even at Morgan Stanley, which unlike most of Wall Street is still highly profitable, the joke is: What's the difference between Salomon Brothers and Morgan Stanley? About six months.

The crash of the stock market is not to blame for the layoffs—just the opposite. There would have been even more cuts if the market had *not* collapsed. Collapse brought an increase in business that always accompanies stock market volatility. Previously redundant employees were suddenly useful hands on the deck during the storm. What is driving the cuts isn't anything so ephemeral as bad markets. It is the mind-boggling growth of investment banks.

That growth began when people like Salomon Brothers chairman John Gutfreund decided that American investment banks had to be either "global" or "niche" players. Being global involved, possibly, doing unprofitable business, because it meant providing all services. If you had told Gutfreund six months ago that he soon wouldn't have a money-market department, he would probably have laughed you off his trading floor. Global meant one dealt in money markets, and in so doing harnessed that mythical corporate force: synergy. When a big institution like the IBM pension fund moved money, a bank wanted to be able to accommodate both sides of the transaction. The money-market business was low margin, but the stock market business was fat, and the old wisdom had it that a bank was less likely to do the one without the other.

Then the global investment banks began to lose money, and the old wisdom flew out the window. Being global is a concept that changes daily, said Salomon Brothers president Tom Strauss when he announced the cuts. Salomon and others will no longer stand money losers, global or otherwise. The irony is that just after Salomon cut its money-market people, the stock market crashed, and

there was a panicky rush of funds into money markets. One Salomon trader griped, "We missed billions of dollars of lucrative business in one day because we didn't have a money-market business any
longer."

Why did a previously profitable business all of a sudden
become unprofitable? Competition. American commercial banks
and Japanese security houses are the villains. Neither of these new
competitors pays their employees anything near what American investment bankers receive. A Japanese banker, as a rule of thumb,
earns his age times a thousand U.S. dollars. The commercial banks,
used to living with much lower returns on capital, effectively
spoiled the municipal market for the likes of Salomon by driving
down profit margins. The Japanese, who have money to burn, have
similarly spoiled the Euromarkets. Like autoworkers and steelwork-
ers, investment bankers are losing their more exalted version of the
American dream because there are people willing to do the same job
for much less pay.

The tragedy of the redundant investment bankers is that, by
their own admission, they don't know how to do anything else.
Sure, there is the odd lawyer, engineer, or even doctor who trickled
into investment banks after learning it paid three times more to sell
bonds than to try cases, build bridges, or transplant kidneys. But
most investment bankers have never been anything else, and are at a
loss for alternatives.

And because they've been so fortunate till now, they don't even
get much sympathy. When a steelworker is fired, friends gather
round—perhaps handing him Rabbi Harold Kushner's *When Bad
Things Happen to Good People*—and shake heads together at the in-
justices of this world. When an investment banker is fired . . . well,
nobody's quite sure what to feel—possibly glee. *When Bad Things
Happen to Rich People* hasn't yet been written.

Euphoria has been the general response of the media. In England, the *Independent* has dubbed Salomon Brothers the Hunger-
ford Brothers, in reference to a recent mass murder in the English
town of that name. The *Spectator* labeled the victims "puppies"
(previously urban professionals). And journalists in City of London
restaurants have been overheard ordering "Smoked Salomon," then
laughing at their own joke.

Investment bankers are supposed to be prepared for their own undoing, but they aren't. From what I have seen, young investment bankers haven't been stuffing their fat bonuses into bank accounts. They've been spending it as fast as it comes in. The Harvard Business School textbooks say that one reason American investment bankers have been so highly paid is to compensate them for low job security. But this was only theory. Nobody took it to heart.

People in
Glass Penthouses...

Towards the end of *Surviving at the Top* the reader actually feels something like pity for the hero. This brief, unlikely moment occurs when Trump is describing his bizarre dealings with Leona Helmsley. Long ago, he explains, the middle-aged Leona took an uncommon fancy to him:

> For some reason [writes Trump], even though I was not tremendously successful at the time, Leona always liked having me around. . . . I was always asked [to be at her parties] and was always given a seat, usually right near her.

Trump has already alluded several times to his own sex appeal and once claimed that "I've never had any problem in bed." Once again the air grows steamy and windows begin to fog, and for a delicious moment the reader savours the image of Trump and Helmsley romantically entwined (imagine the battle for the third pillow!). Then the worm, as it were, turns. The young and dashing Donald escorts a fashion model to one of Leona's parties. Leona flies into what appears to be a jealous rage. "How dare you bring that tramp to one of my parties," she screams, in the presence of the other woman. "At first I was shocked," says Trump, "but then all the things people had been telling me about her Jekyll-and-Hyde personality started coming back to me." From then on Leona, with her "crazed personality," heaps all manner of abuse on Trump. "On two occasions," he writes, "she actually gave me the finger across a crowded New York ballroom."

This rare passage in which Trump seems at the mercy of forces beyond his control ends quickly. The roles reverse when Trump steamrollers over Helmsley in a deal, then fires off a few gratuitous insults of his own. Trump, once again, is the Conqueror.

Filled as it is with Trump's usual commercial sado-masochism, *Surviving at the Top* is already out of date. Trump can no longer afford to insult at will. He can no longer sow salt into the real estate of his enemies. We now know that Trump's business, premised as it was on rising property prices and foolish bankers, has collapsed. He is losing money. He is a virtual slave to external forces. With his debts exceeding his assets by as much as $250 million, his bankers watch and advise his every move. He has had to agree, for example, not to spend on himself more than $500,000 a month. Yet he still insists, like a captured tyrant, that he is in charge.

Reading the scene between Trump and Helmsley, I began to wonder if there isn't something in the Manhattan soil that drives those who wish to control it to distraction; it is not just Leona who has gone loopy. The book Trump has presided over is full of petty, desperate, and often risible swipes at anyone who has ever dared to criticize Donald Trump. Of a *Village Voice* writer named Wayne Barrett, Trump says: "Barrett, whose last book was a major failure, is still trying to make his name at my expense." Of a piece in *Forbes* estimating (generously, it turns out) his net worth at a mere $500 million: "Who can say what these one-of-a-kind-assets are worth until they are put on the market? Certainly not some mediocre reporter from *Forbes* named Richard Stern." Of Garry Trudeau's widely loved Doonesbury cartoons in which Trump was lampooned: "Trudeau's wife, Jane Pauley, is much more talented than he is."

Trump's relentless accumulation leads people often to mistake his motive for greed, when what drives the man is more a pathological need for control. But control of what? Perhaps there was a time when he wanted to control his business; now he seems merely to want to control the opinion others hold of him. Trump has come to believe that if he nurtures his fame, his business will follow. "Success," he writes, "is so often just a matter of perceptions." That may explain why he goes berserk when a journalist tries to tinker with his image, but it still represents an odd and (it now seems) wrong-headed approach to commerce. The man whose first impulse after he buys a building is to change the façade has himself become nothing but a façade. And his book is a strained, sloppy exercise in restoration.

Trump begins the job by gluing upon himself the best tinsel and chrome that money can buy. There are half-a-dozen photographs in *Surviving at the Top* of Trump with celebrities of the moment (Hulk Hogan?) who do not even appear in the text. Trump devotes a chapter to his friendship with Mike Tyson without ever explaining how it began. The rest of the book is a blizzard of name-dropping. The index starts with Ali, Muhammad and ends with York, Sarah Ferguson Duchess of. In between there are perhaps ten names not recognisable to readers of *People* magazine: under "V", Vanderbilt family and Van Gogh, Vincent; under 'O', Onassis, Jackie. "Pick the wrong name," says the author in explaining why he named a casino Trump, "and no matter what else you do you'll never be a hit." (Perhaps there's a new Trump board game in this: I give you a letter from Trump's index and you guess who is listed underneath. Pick the wrong name and I foreclose on you.)

Another stratagem in Trump's bag of cheap building tricks is simply to tell us repeatedly how widely loved and admired he is. Of a trip to Brazil (a country with which he has much in common, financially) he says only that "I found Brazil to be a lovely, if economically troubled, country. And I was surprised and delighted that children came running up to me with pencils and paper yelling, 'Mr. Trump, Mr. Trump.' " He walks down Fifth Avenue and

about 25 perfect strangers wave and shout, 'Hi Donald,' and 'How're you doing Donald,' and 'Keep up the good work.' One thing this proves to me is that the average working man or woman is a lot better adjusted and more secure than the supposedly successful people who stare down at them from the penthouses.

So says the penthouse dweller. And he may be right (all the best theories of human behavior include oneself). *Surviving at the Top* is

a portrait of an ego gone haywire. The madness of the author is its
dominant, if unintentional, theme. He saves the reviewer a paragraph transition by raising the issue himself. "I'm not the same person that I was just a few years ago," he writes early in the book, "and
the changes I've undergone are the subject of this book." In a chapter called "The Survival Game," he suggestively offers a list of once
wealthy men who died by suicide; they are, it seems, his bogey. He
compares himself to Howard Hughes:

> As time goes on I find myself thinking more and more
> about Howard Hughes and even, to some degree, identify-
> ing with him. Take, for example, his famous aversion to
> germs. While I'm certainly not as fanatical as he was, I've
> always had very strong feelings about cleanliness. I'm con-
> stantly washing my hands. . . .

But he is not exposing himself so much as shopping for new
identities. Having tried Howard Hughes (or Lady Macbeth) on for
size, he at last selects another, equally implausible shell. He tells us,
in so many words, that he has discovered the futility of the possessions he calls "my trophies." The best known of these is perhaps the
yacht, now named the *Trump Princess*, purchased from the arms
dealer Adnan Kashoggi (see Doonesbury for details). Trump
devotes a chapter to the *Princess* identical in tone and content to the
braggadocio in "The Art of the Deal": how brilliantly Trump haggled for it, how Trump's boat is the biggest, how Trump made it
better, and so on.

Then he lobs in his newly acquired knowledge of himself:

> But as much as I've enjoyed it until now, and as impressive
> as it has been to my casino customers, I think I'm giving
> up the game of who's got the best boat. . . . It's funny how
> the boat seemed more appropriate to my life in the past
> than to my future.

It is even funnier that this decision comes at just the moment he can
no longer afford the boat. There's every reason to believe that self-
denial is just one more gewgaw for the Trump façade, stuck on to

distract us from the quality of the workmanship. After all, the man has built a career gloating over his ability to fool others; "fool" comes second only to "loser" as Trump's favourite epithet. The truth is more likely to be that if his real estate recovers, the man will begin bragging more loudly than ever about his boat. But who then will listen? Only his ghost.

Milken's Morals
and Ours

The perversity of the public prosecution of Michael Milken was that it ignored what troubled people most. Probably, there is someone out there who turns purple at the mere thought of a man violating a half dozen of the more technical rules in our stock markets (as Mr. Milken did); there is probably someone who believes jaywalkers deserve the death penalty.

But sensible people were far more upset that Mr. Milken had helped to buy and mince America's largest corporations—while earning himself a billion or so dollars. He seemed to mock the widely cherished notion that the market is sensible and just, and was as annoying as a double-parked Rolls-Royce.

Today's sentencing* of Mr. Milken—added to the $600 million fine he has already agreed to pay—is meant to be a kind of moral resolution. The villain is being punished, once again proving that mocking American capitalism doesn't pay. But there are several reasons why this ending should trouble people who like their morality tales neat.

The first is that, of Mr. Milken's many disruptive deeds, none that truly angered people was illegal. Selling junk bonds to willing investors—even to savings and loans—was legal. Handing the proceeds to Ronald Perelman, Nelson ("if you aren't born with it, you

*Mr. Milken was sentenced 21 November 1990.

have to borrow it") Peltz, and Carl Icahn, who wished to dismantle America's largest corporations, was also legal. Even earning $550 million in a year was legal. And make no mistake about it: no more than a few of those dollars can be traced to Mr. Milken's crimes.

Moreover, the people who matter—the raiders and their bankers—still feel the takeover craze was, on balance, good for the economy. Thus, we are still unclear about the ethics of the important part of Mr. Milken's behavior. Anyone who doubts this must explain why, after the collapse of Mr. Milken's employer, Drexel Burnham Lambert Inc., nearly every Wall Street firm rushed to hire his former cronies.

Mr. Milken's defenders say that his junk bonds filled a hole caused by the folly of America's leading bankers and provided money to companies that needed it. The takeovers he funded forced corporate executives to trim fat. Perhaps Mr. Milken and Drexel forced the issue a bit and arranged a few takeovers that should never have occurred. But so did everyone else on Wall Street (if you really want to see damage to the economy, visit Salomon Brothers, which created a string of disastrous leveraged buyouts).

We have prosecuted the man but ignored his ideas. Sometimes the man embodies the idea well enough to justify such a procedure: Michael Deaver, the former aide and confidant to Ronald Reagan, pretty much captured Washington influence peddling, for example. But Mr. Milken is a poor stand-in for Wall Street Greed.

For a start, he thought what he was doing was right. Unlike most of Wall Street's leading deal makers, he genuinely believed he had a mission to reform the American economy. He lived modestly ("I have one house, one wife, one cat, one car," he once said, truthfully). He didn't gloat like Ivan Boesky or preen in public like Donald Trump. He was revered by his employees and devoted to his family (to the extent that he sacrificed himself to exonerate his brother). In short, if we had to go after a man instead of an idea, we could have found a better specimen.

The moral of the Milken story isn't that greedy people always suffer a comeuppance; you have only to look in the mirror to see that isn't true. The moral is that people who force unwanted change on other people—particularly those with power—should always keep a lawyer on hand. Mr. Milken showed how disruptive a genuinely gifted financier could be. On balance, I think, we'd prefer our bankers a little stupid.

It is our dirty little secret that, even as we congratulate ourselves for the wonders of our economic system, we disapprove of many of its natural outcomes. As a wealthy investment banker friend of mine put it, "There is something wrong with making $550 million in a single year." In the end, Michael Milken mocked not only capitalism but our faith in it, too.

Horatio Alger
Trumped

In the past couple of years the agile rich have performed a neat spiritual U-turn. Amid collapsing asset prices and a shifting zeitgeist, the Bible seems to have replaced *The Art of the Deal* as the class text. Ivan Boesky has claimed he wants to become a rabbi, Michael Milken has escorted poor children to baseball games, and scores of young, unindicted Wall Street drop-outs have said that they intend to earn less money and lead more socially redeeming lives. Even Donald Trump in his most recent memoir makes loud noises about the futility of material possessions.

All of which is as human as it is convenient. For almost ten years, however, the lucky winners of the Reagan years sent a quite different message to the less fortunate: success was money, and money was made with debt, tax games, paper shuffling, and arrogance. The people listened. And an insidious side effect of the chrome-plated Reagan boom may yet to be fully realized: the average American has been left with a whole new notion of how to succeed.

The man who is at once the voice and beneficiary of this new idea is named Charles J. Givens. For the past few years Givens has been hawking to ordinary Americans a way of life redolent of the financial '80s. His book, *Wealth Without Risk,* has sold more than a million copies and has been stuck at the top of the Advice and How-to Best-seller Lists for the past eighty weeks. He has been advanced $3 million by Simon and Schuster for a sequel. He has started an organization, named for himself, which has a quarter million members and is growing more quickly than ever. And he has been featured in such putatively respectable organs of business as *Success* magazine, a sure sign something is amiss.

Givens first reaches his audience with a series of late-night, fifteen-minute television commercials. A white stretch limousine glides across the screen as Givens restates the generous American belief that it is never too late to remake one's character. "The last four letters of American are I CAN," he says. "Everybody can be a winner. . . . You don't need to have big money to make big money. . . . All you need to be is serious about wanting to be wealthier. . . . Come to see us and it may change the rest of your life." Givens appears—in a photo with George Bush and clips from virtually every talk show in America—and a second voice enters to establish his credentials as a Success merchant: "Although Charles Givens started out with nothing, today he is accustomed to moving in the centers of power." Then the voice begins to tick off Givens's possessions, as if these, too, were credentials: his "$150,000 Rolls-Royce and stretch Lincoln"; his "$2 million Florida tree-lined estate"; his "staff of six"; his "candlelight dinners" eaten from his "$50,000 antique dining room set."

At first this seems like just a more crude and commercialized version of such premodern merchants of success as Dale Carnegie *(How to Win Friends and Influence People)* and Norman Vincent Peale *(The Power of Positive Thinking)*. But then we hear how several average Americans have found Success with Charles Givens. A man described as "possibly the richest fireman in America" says, "At the time [before he found Givens] we were paying taxes like everyone else. Then we went into the 0 percent tax bracket." Another man mentions how he reduced the interest rates on his credit cards. Givens himself says that the way to succeed is to "start by making everything you spend money on tax deductible." The advertisement attracts people to Givens's free lectures, where new members are enrolled at $499 a head in the Givens Organization.

I traveled to Queens for one of the dozen talks given recently in the New York area. More than 2,000 undersuccessful people filled an auditorium on a rainy week night to hear one of the many Givens spokesmen now touring the country. Right from the start the event had quasi-religious overtones. The speaker was introduced by his proud, sparkling wife, much like a Bible Belt television preacher. His creepy Aryan charm recalled the representatives of "Up With People," who do half-times at the Cotton Bowl. He said so often that he "cared" about us and that he wanted to "share" his success that it was easy to forget you were expected to pay for the privilege. Like Givens, the speaker was a poor boy made good; he had once, he said, held a job that paid him a dollar an hour to count nails. So there was hope for us all. "The difference between *you* and everybody else," he told us with a Baptist twang, "was that you *cared* enough to take that first step."

God and money have never been as far apart in America as they are in most places. Partly this must be because selling is a form of ecstasy in America. But there is also a long history of American preachers aiming to reconcile the moral precepts of the Bible with the making of money. (Peale is one example, as was Russell Conwell, the author of the world's most successful success pamphlet, based on a sermon, called *Acres of Diamonds.*) With the clergy dragging God toward the market, it seems only practical for the laity to pick up the market and drag it toward God. Thus the new breed of success merchants laces its language with pulpit-speak and references to Christian values.

"I'd like to *share* with you," said the speaker, "the strategies that the rich and the wealthy and the elite have been using for years." And with that he moved to the meat of his lecture, which assumed an income of about $20,000 a year. (The crowd seemed comfortable with this assumption.) The speaker started with a reevaluation of the credit card. He revealed that there was a credit card issued by a bank in Arkansas bearing an interest rate of only 11.75 percent. A murmur ran through the crowd. The Givens Organization tracks credit card interest rates around the country, so Givens members can always be using the card with the lowest rate. But that's not the Credit Card Strategy. The Credit Card Strategy is to find a card with no up-front fee and a long grace period. With the card you borrow interest-free money, then deposit that money in an interest-bearing account. "It's called the float," said the speaker, "and it can earn you up to $400 a year.... Using other people's money is what the float is all about."

Nobody laughed. Here was a way to make money without working or taking risk! he enthused. Just like they do on Wall Street! he might have added. The credit card with a grace period is a vehicle by which every American can become a banker. It is also deeply anti-social: it only works as long as a small fraction of the issuing bank's clientele practices the strategy. The "float" is money borrowed interest-free from the issuing bank, and a bank that makes loans free of interest can't survive. Like a lot of the high-rolling strategies of the 1980s, this trick exploits to the hilt the gap between what is legal and what is right. In a funny way it is reassuring that the average guy has come to appreciate that there is some trick to success, that success as we now know it is less a product of industry than of beating the system. What more could one ask of people whose bank managers gamble with their deposits? On the other hand, the attitude underpinning the Credit Card Strategy is a social problem that, like rising crime and street people, can plausibly be dropped on the doorstep of the Roaring Eighties. As if to illustrate my point, the speaker removed his jacket-with-pocket-handkerchief, revealing (I swear) a pair of red suspenders. Clearly the style of the newly rich has trickled down faster than their money.

"The average American makes about $350,000 over a lifetime," continued the speaker. "If we could save some of those dollars, think how much richer we'd be. That's why we need tax strategies." The first strategy was to start a small business. Not actually to *do* anything, mind you. A business, he said, was a tidy package of twenty-seven different legal tax deductions. It enabled you to deduct, for example, the allowance you pay your kids ("Pay 'em to answer the phone, to wash the company car"). It enabled you to take friends out to dinner on Uncle Sam ("So long as you discussed business before, during, or after the meal with this customer who happens also to be a friend or a neighbor . . . after all, they too can be customers"). But best of all, "There's no minimum number of hours you have to spend on this business. You don't have to quit your job." In sum, "Starting a small business can make those dollars you are already spending *tax deductible.* "

The second strategy, really just more of the same, was to deduct all your time spent away from your new business. "Your vacations," he said, "are tax deductible." Arrange to be interviewed for a job with Caesar's Palace (wink, wink), and a trip to Las Vegas can be passed off as business. The crowd chuckled with delight. "Oh," he said, growing emotional, "there are just a *bunch* of things like this I wanna share with you." And who could blame the people for listening? Not Henry Kravis, who made his first billion structuring leveraged buyouts, the success of which turned on tax schemes; not Donald Trump, who explains in *The Art of the Deal* how he made his first big killing by squeezing a forty-year exemption of property taxes out of the city of New York.

Of course, none of these two-bit schemes adds up to real wealth, just a bit more pocket money. What Givens is selling isn't so much success as the illusion of success. But even this is a reflection of the times, when success for the average person has become chiefly an illusion created by the not-so-average person. So says the past master himself. "Every blue-collar worker wants to be treated like a high roller, not like an ordinary guy," writes Trump about his troubled casino. "These people gravitate towards the symbols of success; they want to TOUCH success. Knowing this, I wasn't surprised when [a neighboring casino's] blue-collar ad campaign turned out to be a total failure."

In his slightly out-of-date but otherwise excellent study, *The American Idea of Success*, Richard Huber traces the development of three distinctly American paradigms of success. The "character ethic" is the neglected idea that one gets ahead by application and thrift. The "mind-power ethic" is Peale and all those people who listen to tape recordings in their sleep. The "personality ethic" is the graduate of the Dale Carnegie course, who insists on using your name at every turn ("Remember," wrote Carnegie, "that a man's name is to him the sweetest and most important sound in any language"). The last two, creations of modern American capitalism, are easily mocked; yet both have their redeeming sides. The modern idea, which might be called the "financial manipulation ethic," does not. Or if it does, I haven't been able to find it.

Givens, oddly, claims to follow in the tradition of Dale Carnegie. In the success he has enjoyed he may be right. But in the spirit of the success he has been selling he couldn't be further from the truth. This was made plain at the end of the lecture in Queens, when people went out into the foyer to join the Givens Organization.

Perhaps 400 of the 2,000 in attendance were inducted. Given the preternaturally loving tone of the lecture, the process was surprisingly contentious. Ten Givens men with blow-dried hair, false smiles, pocket handkerchiefs, and red suspenders stood behind tables and told prospective members that the minute they left the building the price of membership would rise from $499 to $599. The people argued and haggled, prompting a Givens man to sprint back into the lecture hall (where the speaker was answering questions) and grab the speaker's proud wife. "You gotta come help," he said, "things are getting ugly. These folks are rude and *irate.*" Where, he might have asked, is Dale Carnegie when you need him?

Taken for a Ride
on the
Customer's Yacht

Here is how it started. Not long ago I was paging through the back section of the *Wall Street Journal* when I was halted by a strange little advertisement, which is to say that it had nothing to do with fiber optics, biogenetics, or choosing a tax-free portfolio. "Financial Seminar at Sea: Explore the Amazon with Louis Rukeyser," it read. My first reaction was . . . well, I'm not sure what my first reaction was. Maybe that "Wall Street Week" 's droll host, America's most durable television host after Mr. Rogers and Johnny Carson, was the victim of an even more droll practical joke. In any case, I put it out of my mind and continued my quest for the program-trading news of the day.

Two days later I came to my senses and fished the paper out of the garbage. I dialed the toll-free number and reached a woman who swore not only that the money boat was for real (200 people had signed on, at an average cost of about $4,000 each) but that it was even something of a tradition. Every year since 1980 a group of American investors has struck out on the high seas with Louis Rukeyser, though never before had the investors followed Rukeyser into the jungle. The Greek cruise ship *Stella Solaris* would start in Barbados and finish ten days later 1,000 miles up the Amazon in Manaus, Brazil. But no matter how many incredulous sounds I made, the woman on the phone refused to see anything weird or funny about people hacking their way into South American rain forests to talk about their portfolios. "They want to learn how to make money on Wall Street," she said, as if the thing couldn't be more plain.

"What kind of people go into the Amazon to learn how to make money on Wall Street?" I asked.

"Oh," she said, "*all* kinds of people: doctors, lawyers, accountants."

She was happy to send me the promotional literature, even though I wasn't, by this logic, a kind of person. It included a pamphlet called *Cruising: Answers to Your Questions,* a list of prices, a list of speakers, and a colorful brochure. The pamphlet answered all my questions as well as a few that hadn't occurred to me ("Will I gain weight?" "Will there be people like me?" "Will I get bored?"). The brochure spoke of "VIP service," friendly get-togethers with "your distinguished fellow investors," and "a personal memento photograph" of you with Louis Rukeyser. It was illustrated with two photographs: one of a smiling Mr. Rukeyser in his Brooks Brothers suit; the other of a bare-chested Amazonian tribesman with a spear in his hands, a two-foot feathered ornament in his nose, and seven-inch, superstretched decorative earlobes. Above the pictures were the words: "Launch Your Investment Strategy for the 1990's with America's Top Financial Experts."

That settled it. I was going. All I needed was a few tubes of jungle formula insect repellent, a box of malaria tablets, the usual inoculations (typhoid, yellow fever, hepatitis), and an HP 12-C hand computer (to calculate yields).

I considered also the matter of a traveling companion. Most of the great Amazonian explorers—from the conquistadors to Sting—had taken traveling companions. The problem was that none of my friends who worked on Wall Street cared enough about Louis Rukeyser to follow him into the jungle. No one watched his show. One dismissed the whole trip with the assertion that Louis Rukeyser was "for old people." I realized that in spite of having spent three years on Wall Street, I knew of only a single member of the reputedly devoted audience of Wall Street's most popular television show. He was available, but I wasn't sure that my mother would let him go.

I called my father and suggested, rather touchingly I thought, that a ten-day journey offered a father and son a chance to talk about the important things in life—like estate planning.

He wasn't interested.

I tempted him with the historical importance of the event. Each nation, I said, has gone into the Amazon in pursuit of its private obsessions. If the Spanish had gone in search of El Dorado, followed by the British in search of bug species, followed by Brazilian city slickers in search of raw materials, wasn't it natural and fitting that Americans in our time should go into the Amazon in search of investment advice?

"You sound like a bad magazine article," he said.

So I dangled before him the prospect of having his picture taken with Louis Rukeyser.

"Who are the other experts?" he asked.

That was the catch. Like about half of America, my father believes he can systematically beat the stock market; it is his wisdom and experience that give him the necessary edge. Shallow pretenders with easy theories who think they too can beat the market bother him. It pleases him to see Rukeyser embarrass the various hemline theorists, 75-year cyclists, Elliott Wavers, and druids who regularly appear on the show to announce that the Dow will break 4,000 during the next harmonic convergence. He doesn't watch Louis Rukeyser merely for the advice on offer. He watches Louis Rukeyser for the same reason every right-thinking, sexually repressed, country club Episcopalian lingered long and hard over the delicious defrockings of Jimmy Swaggart and Jim Bakker. It confirms his skepticism about alternative forms of belief.

So I wasn't surprised that he balked when I read to him the list of pin-striped, right-thinking fiscal bishops who'd be with us on our voyage: Mr. Marshall Loeb, the managing editor of *Fortune* magazine; Mr. A. C. "Ace" Moore, a director of Argus Research in California; and Mr. Hugh Dinwoodie, a stockbroker with the National Bank of North Carolina. A fair cross-section of Wall Street punditry, perhaps, but not enough lunacy for my father's taste.

"That's awful!" said my only hope for a traveling companion. "Call me when they get some Wave people."

29 January: On a Dock in Barbados

The photo session with Rukeyser was scheduled for 9 P.M., and it was nearing 8 P.M. when I sat down on the dock, inoculated against every disease but despair. The dock was deserted. There were half a dozen cruise ships in port, none of them mine. I knew this because I'd walked about five miles with bags to read the names on their sides. It was raining of course.

After about ten minutes of looking lost and wet and pitiful I was approached from the shadows by a Barbadian entrepreneur who offered to rescue me—for a fee. I paid, and he immediately pointed past the sleek white cruise ships that dominated our view to a dark scaphoid form on the horizon. The horizon was actually the end of the dock. The smallish speck was the Stella Solaris. I struggled for a moment with what the psychiatrists call denial.

"If that's my ship, how come there are no people running out to get on it?" I asked.

"Everybody on board," he said. "The ship gets them on so the people don't spend all of their money in Barbados. So they spend it on the boat. Besides, most of them too old to run."

It was 8:30 when I arrived in the Solaris lounge—the center of our lives for the next 10 days—and there was still no sign of Louis Rukeyser or Marshall Loeb. Seated in the lounge were my distinguished fellow investors, the oldest collection of doctors, lawyers, and accountants ever assembled. It was quiet as a funeral; a less charitable observer might say it was well on its way to being a funeral. These were not the sort of old people who inspire cries of "My! They get around for their age!" or "I hope I do as well as that when I'm 75!" These were the sort of old people who make one ask, "Are they breathing?" Their hands were trembling and their eyes were vacant—quavering memento mori. I must have been moved by the determination of these aged conquistadors because I forgot all about the free photograph with Louis Rukeyser, who in any case didn't seem to be around, and sat down among them to watch. As I sat down a Corsican man with a Saddam Hussein moustache appeared on the stage and began to mangle "New York, New York" ("*eef* you can make *eet* there you make *eet* anywhere").

Watching retired people is not very entertaining, in my opinion. Their minds seem to be entirely focussed on the next step their bodies will take. Their humor and wit suffer as a result. When one man in a large group looked out the lounge window and down at the water, another said, "You better watch out for the sharks," and everyone chuckled like it was the best thing that had been said all night. That may explain why they are willing to endure the most appalling entertainment without movement or complaint. But people over 65, for both the heir and the investor, are extremely important. They control 40 percent of the nation's stocks and mutual fund shares. Their tastes, preferences, beliefs and superstitions decide who has access to money and who does not. Old people might not move so well themselves, but if they decide all at once they like a company, they can send its stock up like a shot through the roof.

I was considering this when there was a sudden rush in the corridor of noticeably energetic people wearing little gold name tags. They weren't much younger than the group in the lounge, just more mobile. And at the front of the pack was Louis Rukeyser, suit tailored, hair corrugated, frown fixed in place. He flew past in formation, a middle-aged woman at each elbow. He looked just like George Washington on the face of the dollar bill. But then, everyone says that.

Chasing after him I was stopped by two people. First was a heavyset man who introduced himself as Paul. Paul worked for the travel agent responsible for the ads in the *Wall Street Journal* and, at the moment, controlled access to Rukeyser. He asked where I had been during the free photo session. Before I could explain, he asked if I was the guy who wrote that book about Wall Street. When I said yes, his statements turned into exclamations: "Louis is reading that book! He'd like to meet you!"

Spinning away from Paul, I bumped into Margo, a 52-year-old divorcée and, after me, about the youngest person in the seminar. Margo overheard Paul talking to me and rushed up afterward to announce "that's so great that Louis wants to see you!" She instantly put herself in the role of concerned mother figure, dusting the lint off my jacket, ensuring that my hair was combed, et cetera. "You know Louis never had a son," she said. "I'll bet he always wanted a son."

In the first two minutes of our conversation Margo told me *a)* that the stock market was heading north, *b)* that she feared she wasn't going to spend as much time with Louis as she had hoped and *c)* that Louis was sexy. "I've seen him in a T-shirt, and he's well-built," she said. She wanted to talk to Louis because she had sold naked call options in the stock market and was wondering whether to cover her position. And Louis had a strong view on the market.

Having established that everyone on board knew more about Louis than I did, I headed for my cabin. For no good reason except the basic human desire to rise above my bank account, I had envisaged dark wood paneling, a king-size bed, and maybe a hoot and holler to shout for champagne and stock quotations. Instead my cabin on Ruby Deck had plasterboard walls, a cot, and an opaque port hole. The important thing about Ruby Deck is that it didn't have any rubies. The ship had six passenger decks. The cheapest four had the most expensive-sounding names. A cabin on Sapphire Deck, in the bottom of the ship, where they kept the cooks and the livestock, cost $2,400. After that came, in order of respectability, the Emerald, Ruby, Golden, and Solaris Decks. If you were after cachet, however, you hired a $10,000 double cabin on Boat Deck, at the top. Louis, Margo had said, was on Boat Deck.

30 January: At Sea

Woke up happy and tired: happy because I'd been invited to dine at Louis's table tonight, tired because every time I'd started to drift off I was jolted awake by someone sitting on the end of my bed shouting things like: "Don't you mail letters from this ship?!" It turned out he wasn't on the end of the bed but the other side of my wall. Thin walls saved me the trouble of using the drinking glass to eavesdrop but made it difficult to read my copy of Louis Rukeyser's 1983 book, *What's Ahead for the Economy*. My neighbor shouted everything he said in the fashion of the newly deaf. After we were awakened by the eternally sweet voice of the cruise director, which emanated from the intercom beside our beds, my unseen neighbor began to shout about his stock portfolio. "I could buy 100 and make a little money or buy 1,000 and make a lot of money!" he said. That marked him as one of ours (only about a fifth of the ship's passengers were attending the financial seminar). But who was he talking to? The odd thing about his steady stream of commentary is that it went on without the benefit of reply.

I tried to put a face to the voice as we assembled in the ship's theater for the start of the seminar. We were addressed first by Paul, who for the purposes of this article can be thought of as Louis Rukeyser's bodyguard. His stage manner was a cross between a high school football coach and Stormin' Norman Schwarzkopf. Paul gazed out over the sea of gray heads and announced the schedule in the most weirdly inappropriate tones, as though it were a game plan ("You with the dentures, go deep"). Then he gave us the news, mostly bad.

Marshall Loeb had canceled at the last minute, "to man the war room at *Fortune* magazine." He would make it up to the group by holding a one-hour "briefing session" in the Miami airport, through which most of us would pass on our way home, at the end of the cruise. "Marshall told me to tell you he was very sorry he couldn't be here with you," said Paul. "He says he was a casualty of the war."

The other bad news was that the 200 doctors, lawyers, and accountants I had been promised by the lady on the telephone had been attrited—as they say in wartime—to 69. The final little piece of bad news was that Louis would be leaving for home from Trinidad in the morning. So we should enjoy him while he lasted. The good news was that the Host of "Wall Street Week," Columnist, Author and One of the Ten Best-Dressed Men in the World of Money was present (there he was, right over there in the corner!) and ready to deliver his talk.

The master took the stage. Much of what he said was less applicable to one's portfolio than to one's next vote. Rukeyser is a Reagan Republican, and his talk was partly a therapeutic venting of his spleen against the U.S. government. He offered a rousing defense of the oil companies for raising their prices at the start of the gulf war, a handful of anecdotes, some of which even I recognized from old articles about Rukeyser, and perfectly sensible practical tips like "get your household budget in order," "bring down your debt," and "write your Congressman and insist that he stop stealing from you." The chief danger to the economy was the threat of higher taxes (he advocated a 0 percent capital gains tax). But you get the idea.

Far more interesting than his politics was his approach to personal finance. Absent higher taxes, Rukeyser said, the stock market would rise again and the American economy would recover. He tried to seem self-deprecating at the same time that he reminded us that he had been right all along, both about the direction of the market ("I said the 1980s would be the decade of common stocks") and about specific stocks ("I talked about Compaq when it was at 36, and this morning it is at 64").

The point wasn't that Louis Rukeyser was an investment genius, although that notion was never genuinely discouraged. The point was that the little guy—like him and us—has as much of a chance in the market as "the best minds in American finance." He held up for our total admiration that triumvirate of successful investors, Peter Lynch, John Templeton and Warren Buffet. Louis liked them partly because they were rich and partly because, unlike assorted Elliott Wave theorists and chartists, they were honest enough to admit when they had been wrong. They beat the market not because they had an infallible system but because they had years of accumulated experience and wisdom. They were examples to us all.

When he finished, I realized Rukeyser had done something I had not thought possible. He had, without sounding ridiculous, conjured up a mental picture of Wall Street that in no way would have puzzled a stockbroker or investors who had just awakened from a twenty-year slumber. He never once mentioned junk bonds, takeovers, insider dealing, or the explosion in debt that has defined the last ten years on Wall Street. He never once acknowledged that anything had changed from the good old days (the go-go years, as they are called) when Wall Street was about a lot of small investors picking the right (usually blue-chip) stocks and watching their prices rise. His whole performance was a throwback, as if the financial 1980s had never happened. And it worked. There was a cathartic, spine-tingling moment as he finished, when it felt like a dangerous heresy to even *think* a critical word about Louis Rukeyser. Each and every person in the room was sure that at least four people in America could beat the stock market: Warren Buffet, Peter Lynch, John Templeton, and himself. Rukeyser was paid $25,000 for the speech, which worked out to about $362 for each person in the room. From the response I'd say he was underpaid.

The rest of our day was punctuated by spontaneous motions of approval for Louis Rukeyser. One woman had become so excited she had decided to take control of her portfolio from her stockbroker and said she was going to go home "and tell my broker to take a flying leap." Margo said she was going to hold on to her Schering-Plough. The man on the other side of my bedroom wall shouted that he was going to double his position in General Motors. And so it went.

"I *love* listening to him," said one venerable matron later at lunch.

"Yes," said a gruff fellow whose gruffness was clearly a grand-fatherly ruse. "I enjoyed it too. Can't say I learned anything. But I enjoyed it."

"Oh," said the woman, "I didn't say I *learned* anything."

Later eight of us were invited to join Louis at his table for dinner. Louis, when he appeared, announced that the market had finished up 50 points that day and that the companies he had tipped in his speech (the Gap and Compaq) had seen their stock hit new heights. I had thought Louis might have run out of stories to tell, but no. He was off and running the moment we sat down and didn't stop until I left him (winning) at the blackjack table at 1 A.M. At dinner he was interrupted by devoted followers only twice. The first time he was telling yet another funny story when from across the table a small, previously ignored old man broke in.

"I just want to say one thing," he said a little too loudly.

A few people (including Louis) stopped chattering. The voice sounded familiar to me.

"John Templeton. *Fine* man."

There was an uncomfortable silence. The woman beside him nodded her head, the rest of us offered murmurs of approval, and Louis resumed his story. But a few minutes later the man across the table interrupted again:

"I just want to say one word!"

This time it really was too loud, and everyone went quiet. I know that voice, I thought.

"General Motors. *Fine* company! Real turnaround!"

I introduced myself to Morris Maxwell, my neighbor, the voice on the other side of my bedroom wall. He was pushing 70, and his hearing had gone, but his spirit was intact. His shapely young girl-friend (more power to him) had laryngitis, so she just nodded her head whenever he said anything.

January 31: Trinidad

Louis left. A day of mourning.

February 1: Sick at Sea without Louis Rukeyser

Woke up rested but unhappy: rested because Morris had gone quiet for 24 hours, unhappy because the minute Louis left the boat the sea turned rough. As we steamed across the high seas from

Trinidad to the mouth of the Amazon, most of the passengers were popping Dramamine or pasting Vomex patches behind their ears. The Stella Solaris was taking the swells badly. She tossed and turned in a way that yanked your stomach in two directions at once, as if it were being drawn by wild horses. The ship herself seemed unwell. A woman on Emerald Deck, perhaps the only one healthy enough to care whether she lived or died, told me she was sleeping in her life preserver. The only consolation as I suffered in my cabin on Ruby Deck near the ship's fulcrum was that the fat cats in the suites at the top were probably even sicker than I.

It was about this time that I began to reconsider the purpose of our epic journey: to make money on Wall Street. I confess I had my doubts. The respectability of both stock picking and investment advice has been on a one-way trip south for at least the last twenty years—and maybe since the crash of 1929. Rukeyser, I was beginning to think, might be the last person to persuade five million to ten million viewers each week to tune into the idea that the little guy (or any guy) can systematically outperform the stock market.

My bed rose sharply, as if everyone on board had rushed to the other side.

In the mid-1960s studies came to light showing that professional money managers and stockbrokers had displayed no systematic ability to beat the market. (Similar studies would later show that an investor who took the advice given on "Wall Street Week" did no better than the investor selecting stock at random.) The studies were analytically sound and led in 1973 to the most devastating critique of the professional investment business ever published: *A Random Walk Down Wall Street* by a Princeton professor and former Wall Streeter named Burton Malkiel.

Malkiel first demonstrated the statistical truth of what he called "the narrow form" of random walk, which states that "The history of stock-price movements contains no useful information that will enable an investor consistently to outperform a buy-and-hold strategy in managing a portfolio." In other words, the people who spent their time reading charts of past stock prices (all those Elliott Wavers, hemline theorists, elves, and druids) were wasting their time. Their charts had zero value, except as talismans. That's not to say the chartists would never make money, only that in the long haul they would not outperform the market.

A wave slapped against my porthole.

Of course the debunking of the Holy Rollers tickled every right-thinking Episcopalian in the stock market. The second part of Malkiel's argument, however, was less friendly to the country club set. "Information," he wrote in 1973, "is disseminated too rapidly today, and it gets reflected almost immediately in market prices. By reacting so quickly, the analysts make it extremely difficult to realize a significant profit in the stock market on the basis of fundamental analysis." Thus the value of professional investment advice is zero because all the information on which it is based is already reflected in the market. Wisdom and experience, in other words, stand exactly as much of a chance of beating the market as an Amazonian tribesman blowing darts at section three of the *Wall Street Journal*. Malkiel made gentle sport of the vanity of those who have acquired reputations as market beaters. The big success stories—for example, Peter Lynch, Warren Buffett, John Templeton—were explained perfectly well by the laws of chance. Success in the stock market was no different from success in coin-tossing contests in which those who toss heads are declared winners:

> The contest begins, and 1,000 contestants flip coins. Just as would be expected by chance, 500 of them flip heads, and these winners are allowed to advance to the second stage of the contest and flip again. As might be expected, 250 flip heads. Operating under the laws of chance, there will be 125 winners in the third round, 63 on the fourth, 31 on the fifth, 16 on the sixth and 8 on the seventh.

> By this time crowds start to gather to witness the surprising ability of these expert coin-tossers. The winners are overwhelmed with adulation. They are celebrated as geniuses in the art of coin-tossing—their biographies are written and people urgently seek their advice. After all, there were 1,000 contestants, and only 8 could consistently flip heads. (pp. 164–65)

Everything—"What's Ahead for the Economy," Dramamine, sick bag—skidded off my bedside table.

Anyone who bought into Malkiel's arguments would have fired

his stockbroker and his money manager, and invested his money in stock market indices. He would have canceled his newsletters, sold his pocket ticker tape, reconsidered the amount of time he spent poring over the back of the *Wall Street Journal,* and, in general, start behaving like a citizen of one of those financially sober nations, like Germany. Obviously that did not happen, for several reasons. First, ideas—even wrongheaded ideas—don't die like people. To this day there are thousands of people who believe that there are fortunes to be made from studying charts, just as there are probably thousands of people who believe the sun rotates around the earth. Second, stock market indices are no fun. Textbooks in economics, which explain the economic purpose of money (a unit of account, a store of value, and a means of exchange), usually neglect to mention the chief role of money in America: a source of entertainment. Third, a lot of kind, decent, persuasive people depend for their living on the idea that picking stocks is a plausible road to fortune. This group includes not only stockbrokers, who live on turnover, but money managers such as Peter Lynch, John Templeton, and Warren Buffett, who are paid to pick stocks.

Even Burton Malkiel was not immune to their plight. He apologized to his former colleagues every step of the way as he made his arguments. Then, at the end of his book, he did a curious thing. He confessed his belief that *he* could beat the market. In a heart-warming section called "A Personal Viewpoint" he discussed some of the realities of the marketplace, then concluded: "In such an environment there is considerable scope for an individual to exercise superior intellect and judgment to turn in superior performance."

That left the right-thinking, respectable side of Wall Street with just enough ground to till. On this ground—which is being steadily submerged by evidence to the contrary—Louis Rukeyser makes his living. He doesn't believe in anyone's system, only in the ability of a few hardworking, right-thinking types using fundamental analysis—visiting companies, asking questions, reading balance sheets, et cetera—to beat the market. But if you buy Malkiel's arguments (and there is little reason not to), this notion is every bit as superstitious as the idea that the direction for the stock market depends on the phase of the moon or that you'll get to heaven if you throw rattlesnakes around in church.

I was about here in my heretical thoughts when I finally lurched from bed to the bathroom for an exorcism. Centuries from now, I thought as I leaned to stern, it may be impossible to persuade anyone that they can learn how to make money on Wall Street by venturing into the Amazon with a television personality. After more academic studies and even more fallen idols, we will laugh at stock pickers with the same self-assurance we laugh at those who would cure our colds by applying leeches to suck our blood.

There, that feels better.

February 2 and 3: At Sea

I was at my regular table in the bar when the cruise director announced over the intercom that the president had declared Sunday a national day of prayer. "In view of this," he said, "we will hold a special prayer and hymn service tomorrow morning by the pool on Lido Deck." A woman raised her gin and tonic and offered a solemn toast. "To church," she said. "Praise the Lord," said the man beside her. Others slurred their approval.

Had matters of personal finance not intervened, I believe I too would have spent my morning at a mass baptism on the Lido Deck. Instead I listened to Hugh Dinwoodie, a sixtysomething stockbroker from the National Bank of North Carolina, discuss the rudiments of building a portfolio. Hugh started his speech by telling us how great Louis had been ("I gotta tell you that Louis is getting better and better and better"), thus securing a spot for himself on the next financial seminar at sea. He then launched into his version of how to make money on Wall Street. He played chicken with his subject, racing at it bravely, then veering away at the last moment. He furrowed his brow and looked worried as he offered us hollow generalities, such as "stay away from complicated investments" and "make lists of companies that interest you." I think it was only by mistake that he finished by handing out a list of companies being plugged by NCNB. He watched nervously as we scanned his list with avaricious eyes. Then one of my distinguished fellow investors raised her hand.

"Why did you pick Baker Hughes? They also have a large price-fixing charge to fight. Do you expect them to win?

"Well," said Hugh, fiddling for time. "Good question . . . I'm not saying all these stocks will be winners."

Hugh had the aroma of a stockbroker who had spent too much time in the presence of burning customers. Had he spent any more time on the stage he would have triggered the ship's smoke detector. He was too good-hearted to be intentionally dishonest or venal (few brokers are). But he was too battered by experience to be genuinely optimistic about the possibility we little guys would make money from his advice. Hugh, like a lot of older stockbrokers, had been reduced to the role of professional griever, ready to hold people's hands and weep conspicuously when required. The subtext of every word he spoke was "You may be well and truly reamed by the stocks we at NCNB recommend, but you can rest assured that I will feel worse than you when it happens." Later, when asked what he thought of Eastman Kodak, he shifted uneasily, as if the name evoked bad memories. "For those of you that own the stock," he said, "I've had the pain and suffering along with you." A number of my distinguished fellow investors, it turned out, were clients of Hugh.

The ranks of the seminar were thinning, and there were signs that people were taking it less seriously now that Louis had left. Margo was there, but she'd stopped obsessing about Schering-Plough. Morris still turned up, but instead of his natty slacks and sweater he wore a blue vinyl tracksuit with yellow go-faster stripes and was inclined to sleep. I'd sit behind him (I felt I had an investment to protect) and watch him scrawl at the top of his yellow legal pad *Building your own portfolio,* before he drifted off into a never-never land filled with John Templetons and General Motors and stock splits. Even though he'd woken me almost every morning with his shouting *("You can't lose $2,000 in an IRA!"),* I was finding Morris increasingly lovable. He enjoyed his life.

The no-shows had turned their attention from the seminar to the Amazon. Their leader was no longer Louis Rukeyser but Captain Loren McIntyre, who lectured us daily on the joy of jungle walking. Years back he had spent a year tracking the Amazon to its source, which had been named after him. He had spent months living with Amazonian tribes. He still struck out (aged 74) into the jungle, armed with pen and camera. He wrote books. He had a pet monkey back home in Virginia. He told wonderful stories. He jogged around Boat Deck in the evenings. Ten minutes into his first appearance in the ship's theater, he had stolen the heart of every lady on board.

So as we approached the equator, the balance of reverence of our ship tilted away from the financial gurus. With each tale of derring-do the stock of Captain McIntyre rose and the stock of Louis Rukeyser fell. A little thrill ran through the ship as we learned how to climb into jungle hammocks, to recognize the call of wild birds, to make lists of the equipment we'd need to strike out on our own. At the same time, my fellow investors began to complain: Louis hadn't spent enough time with them; Louis hadn't invited them to the private cocktail party the second night; Louis had been rude to members of the crew. Toward the end of our sea passage I caught two women staring out over the railings, carping about the man who just three days before had held them in his thrall.

"Every year he says the market is going up," said one. "He's bound to be right sometimes."

"Did you hear about his bed?" replied the other.

The bed, the *king-size* bed: A ship is like a small village; there are no secrets on board. Word had spread (even to me, and I seemed to be the last to hear everything) that Louis always demanded a king-size bed on his cruises. He'd been upset to find that his Boat Deck suite was furnished with a queen-size bed. And for the better part of the first day occupants of the other Boat Deck suites were entertained by the sounds of Greeks hammering an addition onto Louis's bed.

"I heard about the bed," said the first. "Did you hear about the orange juice?"

Louis also demanded *freshly squeezed* orange juice. If it came from a can, he sent it back.

Eventually I stopped eavesdropping and asked these two women what was the problem. Oh, they said, there wasn't a problem. No, no problem. They were enjoying the seminar. They just didn't like the way Louis had treated Captain McIntyre.

"What did he do to Captain McIntyre?" I asked.

They wouldn't say. They hadn't *seen* the incident themselves (others had), so they weren't going to repeat it. When I pressed them for details they gave me the same a-lady-doesn't-tell look my grandmother did whenever I asked her if she'd dated anyone before she met my grandfather. So I let it lie. As I say, a ship is a village. Sooner or later someone would tell me what Louis had done to Captain McIntyre.

February 4: Crossing the Equator

The equator is overrated. You can't see it. You are not even on it long enough to conduct a proper experiment. I had wondered how water drains down the sink on the equator, and I'm still wondering. It drains clockwise in the northern hemisphere. It drains counterclockwise in the southern hemisphere. But what does it do on the equator? Does it just sort of sink straight? Even better: Does it not drain at all? And does Louis Rukeyser work only in the northern hemisphere?

February 5, 6, and 7: Avoiding the Jungle

The seminar ended as we entered the river. Ace Moore of Argus Research—a clean-cut, intelligent, honest man loved by all—told us to "follow the example set by Peter Lynch and John Templeton," and some other things too. He revealed no secrets about making money on Wall Street, which was just as well, as there was hardly anyone around to listen. Everyone was out trying to persuade Captain McIntyre to join him for dinner.

Meanwhile Captain McIntyre educated us as to the habits and superstitions of Amazonian tribesmen. The people we call Indians, from Tierra del Fuego to Alaska, though of common origin, have vastly disparate views of the world. One tribe believed their ancestors were jaguars. Another tribe believed the pink dolphins of the Rio Negro metamorphosed into handsome young men and impregnated unmarried girls. While this drew titters from the audience, it struck me as no more absurd than, say, the belief that if you pray hard enough God will give you a Winnebago. yet another tribe had almost done violence to Captain McIntyre when he jogged around their village. The tribesmen believed he was putting a hex on them; when he realized what was happening he reversed directions and unwound the hex. This drew more titters still, and I wondered what the Amazonian tribesmen would think of a people who bought shares in Compaq Computer on the recommendation of a television personality.

Our three days on the river passed without incident. We saw a dead fish, a pet monkey, and, from a great distance, miles and miles of trees. The monotony was punctuated by a single moment of excitement. It happened as we stood on a beach, 900 miles from the mouth of the river, trying to decide which Amazonian tribesman would cut us the best deal on a bulk purchase of T-shirts. There we were—a half-dozen older men and a journalist—balking at the idea of entering the water, when the most senior among us pointed skyward and said, "Vultures."

He spoke in the low tone used by the settler who, crossing the prairie, looks up at the ridge and says, "Injuns."

"Vultures," he said.

There must have been 100 enormous blackbirds circling slowly over our heads as we dabbed our toes in the water. It was the only concentration of life we encountered in a jungle that teems with species. And I don't think anyone in our group would have been more unnerved had he stepped on an anaconda. Captain McIntyre had prepared us for that, at least.

Otherwise we were pleasantly overtrained. Watching the jungle from a cruise ship on the Amazon is not a great deal different from watching the Amazon on television. We espied Amazonian tribesmen only twice—save for the few times they bobbed through our wake in dugout canoes. When we pulled over for a swim, we were assailed on the beach by members of the more entrepreneurial tribes. They sold us fish bones on a string, totems, carnival masks, stuffed piranha, blowguns, T-shirts, and beads. (A Spenglerian might argue that the decline of the West must have begun when we stopped selling beads to the natives and started buying them.) And 1,000 miles from the mouth, docked at Manaus, we were approached again, this time by picturesque small children holding snakes, who sold video rights to their animals.

It was here the story at last emerged. Although I heard bits and pieces every day, I didn't hear it put together until we docked in Manaus. Captain McIntyre sat at his lunch table with four of the more enthusiastic participants in the financial seminar at sea (two women, two men) talking about the Amazon. Then, apropos of nothing, he switched subjects. "You know this fellow Rukeyser?" he asked. We did.

Two days out of Barbados, McIntyre had received an urgent message. His publisher in the States needed a cassette he held on board. The only way to get it there on time was for someone leaving the ship to take it from Trinidad. McIntyre was delighted to learn that a passenger (name of Rukeyser) was heading back. He had never heard of Louis Rukeyser, so he had someone point him out in the dining room.

Rukeyser was at first reluctant. He was busy. McIntyre all but dropped to his knees and pleaded, and at last Rukeyser agreed; he would take McIntyre's cassette and drop it in the first mailbox after he landed in the States. McIntyre then asked Rukeyser to write his name and phone number on a piece of paper, in case something went wrong.

"You mean you don't know who I am?" asked Rukeyser.

McIntyre looked blank. He had no idea. "Who are you?" he asked.

"If you have to ask that, I'm not taking it," said Rukeyser, who then tossed the cassette onto the table and marched out.

McIntyre was sure he had misheard. He stood there stunned. He turned to Paul, who stood, as ever, nearby.

"But he left the cassette," said McIntyre.

"You bet he did," said Paul. "You insulted him."

"How did I insult him?" asked McIntyre.

"You asked him his name," said Paul, perfectly unaware he had delivered one of the greatest lines of all time.

Unfortunately for Rukeyser, McIntyre retold the incident often, with a mixture of amazement and amusement, always leaving the crowd to do the indignation bit. He kept saying how he still didn't know who this guy Louis Rukeyser was. The two women at our table looked sad. The men, on the other hand, erupted with a violence unprecedented by anything that happened on our ship in the entire ten days of the cruise.

"I'm going to write Mr. Louis Rukeyser and tell him he's an asshole!" said number one.

"So he thinks the sun shines up his alley!" said number two.

Later I ran across number one composing a letter, which began:

"Dear Mr. Louis Rukeyser, Some son of a bitch pretending to be you has been behaving in the most disgraceful manner. . . ."

I'm tempted to compare their reaction to that of members of the PTL when Jim Bakker was found out or of the Ministry of God when Jimmy Swaggart was exposed. But it was probably closer to the discovery by Anglican parishioners that the resident bishop had made a pass at somebody's wife. The disillusionment is always proportional in strength to the original illusion; it is the most faithful who are always the most upset. I too was mildly disappointed in Lou, but only because I genuinely liked him. And because at some point, I supposed, I would have to break the news to my father.

February 6: Manaus, 7:00 A.M.

I woke up to find everyone gone. The charter flights back to Miami and the briefing session with Marshall Loeb left early. The boat had emptied of passengers at 5:30 A.M. I lay in bed for a few minutes, getting used to the idea of being alone again and (I admit it) missing the cast of characters I'd been trapped with over the past ten days. It would be a long time before I was surrounded by so many surrogate grandparents. And even if they hadn't really ventured into the jungle, you had to admire them for the enthusiasm of their simulation.

As I left the ship I ran into a young member of the crew who from the start had viewed my incessant note scribbling and interviewing with detached amusement. She couldn't resist a final jab.

"Do you have any more questions—like the weight of the boat or something?" she asked.

In fact there had been one question I had wanted answered from the moment I boarded, but never found the right moment to ask it.

"Do any of your passengers ever die on your cruises?" I asked.

They did. She seemed a bit uneasy about the whole subject. "On one trip to Scandinavia," she said, lowering her voice, "we had to bring two of them back on ice."

"Where do you keep the bodies?" I asked.

"I don't think you really want to know," she said.

"Yes, I really do," I said, because I really did.

"Well," she said, very quietly as if she was about to tell me a big secret, "they have to be kept in a freezer, right?"

"You mean you keep the dead bodies in the meat freezer!" I shouted. But the effect was lost. There was no one around to be shocked.

February 8: Manaus

Couldn't find the local stock market so I decided to call home. My father would want to know all about Louis Rukeyser. After about ten minutes of disputation with Brazilian operators I finally got through to good old AT&T, a company you can only fully appreciate after you've tried to use the phones in the middle of the Amazon (memo to Ms. Drysdale: buy AT&T).

When he came on the line my father, always a happy man, sounded especially chipper. "You'll never guess who called the other day," he said.

"George Bush."

"No," he said, "Louis Rukeyser."

How on earth had he found my father's phone number? I let out a tiny groan.

"He said what a nice boy I had," he continued. "You know, when you grow up and have kids of your own, you'll learn that there's nothing nicer that can happen to you than to have someone call you and tell you your kids are okay. . . ."

I let out a fairly large groan. There was a significant pause on the other end of the line.

"You be nice to Mr. Rukeyser."

PART II

—

OLD WORLD

The brief, torrid affair between British youth and American money receives my vote for the most bizarre and underrated subplot of the last decade, followed closely by the appearance on the financial scene of young Frenchmen who referred to themselves as les golden boys. In the last decade there was a glorious attempt to superimpose an American status system upon an encrusted European class system. Money became more fashionable than birth. Even though I'd lived in London on and off since 1983, I hadn't realized the scope of the development until I published *Liar's Poker* and began to receive letters from young European men and women (but mostly men) who wanted to compare notes. First there was a trickle, then a flood of stories not very different from my own.

It was in the spring of 1984 that Wall Street dealmakers began to view Europe as more than a shopping center. The American firms were expanding rapidly and needed educated bodies to fill the chairs on their trading floors. A few of the more thoughtful Americans were even concerned that demand would exceed supply, that money might not have the same intoxicating effect on European recruits as it did on Americans.

So it happened, in the middle of 1984, that two vaguely uncertain American investment bankers found themselves sitting on one side of a long conference table, facing an applicant from Cambridge on the other. Why, the bankers asked, did an Englishman want to work for the American investment bank?

"I admire your firm's track record and its commitment to excellence," said the student. "The people here are clearly exceptional."

The American bankers agreed. They nearly forgot to be surprised by how eager—how *American*—the kid sounded. "Any other reasons?" asked one.

"I thrive on doing deals," said the student, "and on working long hours. I would view working here not so much as a job but as a way of life. Frankly, working here would put me on a very fast learning curve." *Learning curve?* he thought to himself. That was the American phrase, wasn't it?

"Isn't there something else?" suggested one of the bankers.

"Well," said the student, racking his brain for the crucial lie, the winning lie. "Well," he said "I suppose I *could* use the money."

The bankers looked at each other. There was this awful pause. Then they began to laugh. "Yes," says one, "there's only two groups in town that pay this kind of money. There's us. And there's the Rolling Stones."

I heard many versions of this vignette, but always with the same punch line. I'm told it was all over Cambridge in a week, Oxford in two. The point isn't just that it sounds exactly like about ten thousand interviews taking place at the same time on American college campuses, including one of my own, but that it was retold without a trace of British irony, in a way that was favorable both to the kid and to the bankers. It seems that even the most worldly students at Oxford and Cambridge were unable to resist the offer of such sudden glamor. And so the money culture spread.

Eventually the quest for financial glory by Britain's middle-class college students became one of the most direct challenges ever to British middle-class values. The working class— the coal miners, the Labor party radicals, the 95 percent of the British population that most Americans never see—were never much of a threat to the dons and the barristers. The dons and the barristers could easily ignore envy from below; for some, I'm sure, a little prole envy was one of life's pleasures. But the ridicule of one's children ("How much do they pay you, father? Ha! That's *all??*") was another matter.

The drift of European financiers towards the American value system undermined established class pretensions. Even though the American investment banks tended to hire young men with country homes, they at least paid lip service to the idea of equal opportunity. At Salomon Brothers, anyway, it was not uncommon to find two Englishmen peddling bonds side by side who wouldn't even have *seen* each other had they passed on the street. So on balance—despite the financial havoc they often wreaked—American investment bankers may have been a force of positive social change in the Old World. Who knows, the Committee for a Classless Society in

Britain might one day raise a statue along the Thames of a twenty-two year old Anglo-Saxon in red suspenders waving a cigar with one hand and a fifty-pound note with the other. Then again, it might not.

"Do You Have
a Fire
in Your Belly?"

If you had read the above head-
line as a lead to a recent advertisement in an English newspaper,
what would you have expected to follow?

1.) A sales pitch for a stomach antacid, like Alka-Seltzer.

2.) A tract, in small print, from an obscure religious sect, seeking inflammable men and women passionately to serve a god as
missionaries in the Szechuan province.

3.) A request from an American investment bank for applicants.

You get a gold star if you answered investment bank. The ad
appeared in the Oxford and Cambridge newspapers, and it elicited
hundreds of replies from otherwise fire-resistant Englishmen. For
these are the days when England's educated youth want to be, more
than anything else, American bankers.

So badly do they want this that they are learning to use the
word "aggressive" in the positive American sense of "go-getting,"
rather than the negative English one of "offensively over ambitious." They will memorize the entire starting lineup of the New
York Giants to be fluent in American football when they meet the
American bank personnel director, who is well-known on campus
to be a Giants fan. Or they will practice exposing their ids before a
dormitory mirror. This is the common perception of what is required by American interviewers: the ability to let all of one's pent-
up ambition, raw human greed, repressed needs hang out.

What is sweeping through one square mile of England is the desire to assimilate. But where in the old days American visitors tried, almost instinctively, to blend into English society (J. Paul Getty, up for membership at an English men's club, went so far as to stop talking about his money), it is the young Englishman who is trying to find the rhythm and beat of American business culture.

The young Englishman's goal isn't simply to get in; it's to fit in. Witness one Oxford graduate just home from four months' training in New York: "When Big Bang goes off, we'll be one of the few real players," he says. Asked about his trip, he skips over the bits most Englishmen pause to describe (crime, pushy New Yorkers, the Empire State Building) and gets right to the point: "I never knew my learning curve would be so steep."

Four months ago he didn't know he had a learning curve. American businessmen use the term to describe what happens when their brains are exposed to information over time. The English simply call this learning or, in prolix moments, the learning process. The curve sounds more precise, like something taught in economics classes. Does it slope upward? One hopes. But it can go flat. And people with poor memories could have curves that turn back on themselves, like the Laffer curve. The concept is reassuringly American.

The new prominence of American business culture in England is a product of what has become known as "the Bigger Bang," the enormous increase in the supply of financial services to Europeans by American banks. The term acknowledges that the phenomenon owes something to Big Bang, the deregulation of financial Britain. American banks designated London as their "international headquarters," then proceeded to double and quadruple their London staffs. Their need for educated Englishmen has driven up the price of that commodity. One of the great unanswered questions is why the resulting flood of Englishmen burning to land a job in an American bank hasn't driven the price right back down.

It's just a matter of time before this friendly takeover of English university students gets out of hand. Think about it, say, from the perspective of an American corporate treasurer visiting England for the first time. He's closing his first Eurobond deal, which requires him to visit the American investment bank underwriting his financing.

He therefore arrives in England knowing he will negotiate with Englishmen—the ones who work for the American bank. He is sure that, like Shakespeare and Dr. Johnson, they will be subtle and witty. He prepares for his meetings by reviewing his business school notes on "Cross-Cultural Negotiations," making a mental list of Churchillian quips, memorizing the British kings and queens in sequence, and inventing a joke about Princess Di and Prince Andrew.

He arrives at the offices of Pierce, Stein (a Eurobond firm). A young Englishman greets him. The young Englishman has precisely those qualities sought by American banks in campus interviews: He played competitive sports; he led others; he attended either Oxford or Cambridge; he acts well enough to speak to a Giants' fan seeking naked ids. He could be, for example, Prince Charles.

Prince Charles opens the negotiation briskly. He says, "Here at Pierce we are major players in the Euromarkets. Our real hitters are in M&A; they sure have knocked in a few runs this year."

Our treasurer wants to squeeze in his joke about Prince Andrew—no luck. Prince Charles is pitching Pierce. He boasts about "my innovative idea that resulted in our deal with Widgets & Co. Did you read about it in the *FT* this morning?" Before long, Prince Charles has out his sharp pencil and is selling our treasurer an interest rate swap.

How would you as treasurer respond to this unexpected encounter?

a.) With relief: the English banker isn't as subtle and witty as you feared. The pressure is off. This is the way bankers speak back home, which puts you, perversely, back on your own turf. You lean back in your chair and ask Prince Charles who he likes in the Super Bowl. He likes the "Skins."

b.) With confusion: you had braced yourself for a head-on collision. Instead you get sideswiped. The joke is on you. The time you spent learning English literature, politics, and history has been wasted. You do not waste time lightly. You will close your Eurobond deal anyway, but you will feel it could have been more Euro.

c.) With extreme melancholy and disappointment: face it, you cared less about borrowing money than you did about flying to England to do it. You flew 3,000 miles to witness exotic business behavior—procrastination and learned digressions from port drinking, Cuban cigar smoking, bowler hatted Englishmen. What do you get? Effectively, a guy in a baseball hat eating a McDonald's hamburger who processes you as efficiently as if you were some Eurobond sausage.

The cultural assimilation of Brits will continue. One day American tourists will arrive at Heathrow Airport and find that English taxi drivers no longer speak English or know where to find back streets. The guards at Buckingham Palace won't keep still (they'll smile for photos), and the English bed and breakfast will call itself a motel and raise its price.

Cricket will be for the wimps who can't stomach American football. Sherlock Holmes will be a less muscular version of Bo and Luke Duke from *The Dukes of Hazzard*, and the gardens behind rural homes will become suburban backyards with plastic pink flamingos.

The message is simply this: America will rue the day it infected the educated English classes with American business culture, the day it turned Prince Charles not into a toad, but into Lee Iacocca.

Les Golden Boys

Even as France celebrates the two hundredth anniversary of its revolution this summer,* another revolution is sweeping through its financial markets, well in advance of 1992. The American takeover techniques that Bruce Wasserstein and James Goldsmith have exported to Great Britain aren't going to stop at the English Channel. The insurrectionary contagion is inevitably spreading to France and the rest of Europe, and the Paris Bourse, like the Bastille before it, has already fallen.

Back in July 1987, the first man I met in the Paris Bourse snorted when I asked whether trading on insider information should be a crime. What was the point, he wondered, of trading *without* inside information?

How risky.

How naive.

How—forgive me, monsieur, for saying—American.

There were laws in France against insider trading, he said, but no one paid them much attention. It was said that when people in the enforcement division of the Ministry of Finance got wind of insider dealing and the news was still fresh, they called their brokers. Nobody on the Bourse minded that the stock exchange police were making a killing. Why should they? *Everyone* was making a killing.

He then laughed like a man with a piece of the action and

*September 1989

pointed to the far end of the vast room in which we stood. Across
the floor stocks were noisily changing hands. A middle-aged man in
a white linen jacket, the sort worn by hospital interns and dental
hygienists, lurked in the shadows. He leaned against a pillar, with
the obligatory cigarette in the corner of his mouth. If he hadn't been
flashing buy and sell signals to a man in a gray suit, I might have
guessed he was the Bourse's barber on his lunch break.

And I would have guessed right. "He shaves the beards of the
stockbrokers in the mornings," said my guide, "and hears their news
while he has a razor to their throats. This is why his information is
always pure."

Even after I factored in the delight Parisians take in shocking
Americans, the tale still rang about three-quarters true. The Bourse
in the middle of 1987 was gloatingly licentious, an unpoliced zone, a
place where no one had been caught doing anything wrong for
centuries. Its friends said it had old-world charm. Its enemies said
both it and its denizens needed a bath. The statues of Commerce and
Justice outside the front door had been splattered by generations of
pigeons. The dozen allegories in grisaille on the dome sixty feet over
the trading floor were stained by brokers' nicotine. There wasn't a
computer, a calculator, or a yuppie in sight. When shares in Peugeot
or Lafarge changed hands—at prices fixed each morning by the
brokers—a young lady with more curves than the Mets' pitching
staff erased one number on a chalkboard high above the trading floor
and wrote another. The brokers below, in what seemed to be almost
a reflex action, whistled and hooted. (Women, who were barred
from the Bourse until 1967, were the closest thing in France to a
stock market innovation.)

The men drew their salaries from the forty or so Parisian
stockbrokerage houses, created in 1572 by Charles IX: Baudoin,
Rondeleux, Meeschaert. At the Bourse, each *agent de change* had his
nameplate above his silver hat peg above his silver umbrella box. In
his company brochure, he listed up to four country homes—*residence première, residence secondaire*, etc.—not because he *had* to but
because he *chose* to. His commissions were fixed, his day was short,
his life was good, and he wanted others to know it.

The Bourse was, in short, one of the oldest and most notorious
closed shops in Europe. The notion of a foreigner entering the

French financial markets—much less raiding a French company—
was laughable; you might as well have attacked the Hole-in-the-
Wall Gang in the Hole-in-the-Wall. What was true of France was
also true of Spain, Portugal, Germany, and Italy. American investment bankers hadn't begun to penetrate European markets.

There was a single exception. London, because it felt com-
pelled to compete with Wall Street as a world financial center, had
sacrificed the welfare of its money men and opened its markets.
British brokerage fees were negotiable. A British regulatory body,
called the Securities and Investment Board, was reassuringly similar
to America's Securities and Exchange Commission. When the British stock market began to trade by computer, technology and skill
became more highly valued than a degree from Eton. A lot of old
Etonians went bust or sold out to Americans.

But Paris in 1987 was perhaps the best example of the European
rule: caveat foreigner. The widespread feeling at that time was that a
European Common Market, i.e., a free market, for bonds and stocks
was no more than a nice idea.

Flash forward two years, to July 1989. In the hallway on the
fourth floor of the Bourse, a young French woman whom I'll call
Natalie whispers seductive words into the ear of a Wall Street investment banker. "Here een France," she says, "we have a passion
that does not exeest een England—or anywhere. . . ."

Yes?

". . . a passion for buying and selling financial futures."

Yes! All at once there are the sounds of a thousand half-eaten
chocolate croissants being hurled into trash cans and a mad rush for
the door to the trading room. It is 10 A.M. and *le Matif*, the French
bond futures contract, has commenced trading. Several hundred
twenty-two-year-old French men and women drop their cigarettes—smoking while trading is forbidden—and begin to shout at
the top of their lungs, *"J'ai!" "J'ai!"* (I'm selling, I'm selling) and *"Je
prends!" "Je prends!"* (I'm buying, I'm buying). Over their heads,
ninety-three videodisplay units flash prices. Stunning women in
short skirts run back and forth, yet no man dares applaud. ("They
know I weell heet them eef they wheestle," explains Natalie, one of
the leading futures brokers in the market.)

Natalie, the above-mentioned Wall Street trader, and I sign the guest register and enter. A man steals up behind us to see what we have written.

"He's from Goldman Sachs," says Natalie. "They want to know who are my clients so they can take them away."

Goodbye 1830s and the ancient régime. Hello 1980s and the Wall Street money machine.

Gambling in futures is Paris's latest fashion. In a good week *le Matif* can trade twice the $74 billion the entire French stock market traded in the first six months of this year. French yuppies, called *les golden boys* and *les golden girls,* have replaced the decadent Gaullists of yore. Three of the largest French stockbrokers—Buisson, Baudoin, and Rondeleux—have declared bankruptcy in the last year, two because of speculative losses in futures. Others, cowed by the end of fixed brokerage commissions on stocks (as of July 3), have sold themselves to foreigners or to large French banks. Most of the rest are bleeding money. Taking the winning side of the wild futures trading by the French have been—you guessed it—Salomon Brothers, Goldman Sachs, and Morgan Guaranty.

With the exception of a few oddities, such as the defunct obligations of the last Russian czar, stocks and bonds now change hands outside the Bourse through computer terminals. Negotiated commissions give big institutional investors (bulk buyers who can drive down fees) an edge over private investors. And you can't help but wonder if the trends in the French stock market—frenetic trading, concentration of shares in the hands of institutional investors, and financial entrepreneurship—will lead to an American-style takeover spree as they are doing already in Britain.

Let me explain. The recent multibillion-dollar corporate battles for Gateway, Consolidated Gold Fields, and B.A.T. are no mere coincidences; the current explosion in British takeovers follows directly from the entry several years ago of Wall Street, computers, and competition into the British brokerage business. Changing the structure of the market for corporate shares has profound effects on corporate control for several reasons.

First, when brokerage profits collapse, brokerage firms have to scramble about in order to find new sources of revenues (on Wall Street in May 1975, when fixed commissions were abolished, Joe Perella was encouraged to build his M&A department at First Boston).

Second, when you remove ancient brokerage cartels, you challenge the etiquette of a market. In particular, you disturb the symbiotic relationship between financiers and captains of industry. Once upon a time in Britain, it "just wasn't done" to help James Goldsmith raid BAT. Now it is, partly because the people who used the expression have been replaced by people who don't. And in France, when the old stockbroker becomes a doomed species, the old corporate CEO must wonder if he is next.

The third reason that a stock market free-for-all tends to be followed by a takeover boom is that the second is simply an extension of the idea that created the first: the idea of the free financial market. What has led the French government to ignore the cries of its *agents de change* may also cause it to ignore the complaints of entrenched CEOs: the fear that if it doesn't, Paris will lose financial markets to London—and to any other city in Europe that allows free movement of capital and corporate assets.

That's not to say Boone Pickens will be bidding for the Eiffel Tower anytime soon. Any scramble for French corporate assets will probably be touched off within the Common Market by, say, an Englishman demanding the same right to buy French properties as the French enjoy in Britain. The issue of equal access could easily be the Trojan horse in which European raiders such as James Goldsmith and Italy's Carlo De Benedetti enter France to pursue juicy, undervalued assets. And they will turn to American investment bankers for both advice and money.

Natalie is at first reluctant to take the elevator down four floors and two centuries to the place where, two years before, the barber, the Nation's Razor, made his quick killings. "Nothing happens there anymore," she says, "and the old men say *Ooh la la* if I walk in." Eventually, of course, she gives in to the tourist's entreaties. And in the main trading room of the Bourse, where two years before there had been many hundreds of traders, there are but thirty. The ground floor of the Bourse, including the room with the silver hat racks, is vacant.

The Bourse's main room is called *le Gisement*. "We have an expression in the futures market," says Natalie, "that if you are bad you will go to *le Gisement.*" Financial purgatory.

The Nation's Razor is gone. The Ministry of Finance has begun to crack down on insider traders, albeit gently. Nobody is going to jail anytime soon. But the ministry has, for example, arbitrarily nullified some trades that have occurred immediately prior to the announcement of a takeover. The barber, for all I know, may work from a terminal in his shop. But if I had to bet, I'd say he is sipping a glass of bubbly in one of his homes in the south of France. He looked too shrewd a player not to know when the game is over.

Don't Cry for Me Guacamole

The doors of our jumbo jet emptied into the pandemonium that is now the norm at Sydney airport. Business-class types began their usual time-is-money sprint for passport control, only to run head on into several thousand Japanese schoolchildren with the same idea. Emerging from the rear of the plane, I found myself hemmed in on all sides by Indian women who teetered like Sherpas beneath VCRs, ghetto blasters, and small pieces of furniture. We were like extras in the mass exodus scene in *Gandhi*, and this was *before* we collected our luggage. By the time we reached customs (two-and-a-half hours later), the women were each pushing two trolleys laden with swollen cases. Sprung open by an Australian inspector, these spilled small appliances and wardrobes of exotic clothing.

"How long do you plan to stay in Australia?" the inspector would ask.

"Two weeks."

Now, it is true that some people simply don't know how to travel light, but it is also true that a fantastic number of the putative tourists who squeeze through Sydney's Lilliputian terminal never leave Australia. The streets of Sydney pulse with the same "don't ask me for my green card" capitalism as the streets of Manhattan. This unnerves Australians. They go wide-eyed, like Carl Sagan describing the number of stars in the galaxy, when talking about the number of Asians who want to live in New South Wales. Having spent much of its first 200 years trying to keep people in, Australia seems fated to spend the next 200 trying to keep people out.

Australia's appeal has nothing to do with Crocodile Dundee's bush charm and everything to do with money; you can see this in the time it takes to read a newspaper. The news is dominated by the newly rich, of whom there are a truly fantastic number. The smell of Trump hangs heavy over Sydney harbor. The Trumpian figure best known to Americans is probably Alan Bond, of America's Cup fame. He and his wife, Big Red (no joke), were beamed into my hotel room more frequently than the prime minister: Bond and Big Red stepping into their stretch limo; Bond standing in front of Bond Tower, his Sydney skyscraper; Bond strolling the campus of newly built Bond University; then, best of all, Bond showing off Van Gogh's *Les Irises*. He recently paid $53 million for it, and, instead of feeling dumb, he invited the television crews to his home to brag. Of his new treasure he said, "It's not just a picture. It's the most important picture ever painted."

I didn't sit glued to this by choice. The way I got to Australia was by agreeing to write, for a London tabloid, the definitive piece of hack journalism on Australian bad taste. That's a big subject. The *Bulletin*, an Australian magazine owned, like nearly all Australian magazines, by billionaire Kerry Packer, publishes an annual list of the 100 Most Appalling Australians. Competition is stiff. An oleaginous millionaire with elephants and giraffes in his driveway and two gold Rolexes on the outside of his sleeve ("I must know the time in Paris") wasn't even a runner-up.

The quickest way onto the list, aside from emigrating and becoming famous (Robert Hughes, Olivia Newton-John), is to get money and spend it exotically. Bond and Big Red are, of course, perennially appalling. But they are joined by a rotating cast of hundreds cut from the same bolt of tinsel: Laurie Connell (indicted merchant banker who, à la Milken, has been stripped of his passport), Christopher Skaase (developer known as the *real* Donald Trump of Australia), Warren Anderson (developer who *is* the real Donald Trump of Australia), and so on, ad nauseam. They play polo, shoot small animals from private helicopters, trot the globe in search of antiques and Impressionists, and give their houses names like Fairwater and Notre Dame. And the funny thing is: *they want everyone to know.*

That money is so unabashedly the key to Australian social ambition, and that it talks as loudly in Australia as it does in America, makes one wonder: How does a nation with a left-wing government, a working-class ethic, and a mere 16 million people sustain so many ostentatiously wealthy people?

One answer many Australians give is that the average Australian is so uninterested in economic advancement, and the country is so rich in natural resources (gold, uranium), that any boob who works can make a fortune. Another is that Prime Minister Bob Hawke is much more of a sentimental than a practicing socialist. Even during my stay he was to be found schmoozing the rich. A vicious television exposé alleged that Alan Bond's multibillion-dollar corporation had evaded Australian taxes for years by stuffing its profits away on a nearby island. The story has turned out to be largely true. But on the program Hawke, clearly aware that a left-wing politician can say things a right-wing politician can only dream, said it wasn't his or anyone else's job to question the doings of eminent Australians like Alan Bond.

A few days later, as if to dispel any resulting doubts about his sensitivity, Hawke wept. The newspapers announced he was going to weep the morning before the event. "A tearful Prime Minister Bob Hawke will admit on national TV tonight he has been unfaithful to his wife Hazel," read the lead story in the *Daily Mirror*. "The prime minister will confirm his reputation as a womanizer—but says his straying days are over." What was remarkable about this—to an American at least—was that his confession was entirely unprovoked. He hadn't been tailed. He hadn't been caught John Towering under a restaurant table. He just thought . . . well . . . you know . . . that the people ought to know. Apparently these sorts of confessions elicit a great deal of sympathy Down Under.

After admiring the habits and consequences of rich Australians from afar for a few days, I tried to get closer. It wasn't easy. My London sponsor had victimized these people once too often. The British delight in making fun of rich Australians, and, amazingly, the Australians actually care what the British think. The one brave millionairess who granted me an interview hid her valuables beforehand. There were dust squares on the walls and tan lines on her wrists and neck. She received me in a T-shirt and cotton skirt. The

dead tiger on the floor, she insisted, had *not* been shot by her husband on safari. It had "died of appendicitis."

Luckily, a local (British) gossip columnist tossed me a bone.
Bad taste, he said, loomed nearby. Kerry Packer, Australia's richest
man, had recently imported a string of 100 Argentine polo ponies,
complete with Argentine polo players. The latter were being treated
to a round of parties in Sydney. The Argies, as they were called,
were a triple draw—as sex symbols, as people from a faraway culture
who had no desire to immigrate, and as the guests of Kerry Packer. I
was told that one of these parties, an Argie theme party thrown by
an Aussie coffee mogul, was "important." So I crashed.

The rocks strapped to the necks of the women said I had found
what I was looking for. But I was almost immediately distracted
from determining whether they were real, as it became clear that
something was amiss. A band in sombreros beat out music that
sounded vaguely Mexican. A man dressed to tango handed me a
taco. A pretty blond Australian girl wearing some sort of Aztec
dance costume weaved through the crowd with a plate of en-
chiladas. Someone had made a terrible mistake. None of this had
anything to do with Argentina. The Argentineans, a half-dozen tall
blond men, stood poker-faced in the middle of the room, surrounded by drooling women, swallowing their national pride. Then
the pretty blond girl, making a second pass through the crowd,
reached them. This time she offered guacamole dip. The Argentineans stared down into the lumpy green sludge and burst out
laughing. They said they had never seen anything quite like it.

Then and there something clicked. I had been dogged from the
start by the feeling that I had seen Australia before. Think about it:
vast natural resources, vast tracts of useless land, vast numbers of
provincial rich people, nice weather, lots of cows, constant pressure
on borders from poor aliens, collectors who buy their Monets by the
yard, a robust disrespect for the law, suburban lifestyle, barbecues,
fishy banking practices. It could be only one other place on earth.
But not until the guacamole appeared was I able to put a name to the
place: Te—aw, why spoil it for you?

Portrait of
the American as
a Bond Salesman

Only a month ago I was a be-
draggled American on a hungry prowl through Harrods food halls.
My failures as a bond salesman had turned my platinum American
Express card blue. And my American sales techniques were still
getting nowhere with the British. There and then my fortunes
turned. Now I can buy my salmon and caviar on credit because I've
learned how to sell things—that is, how not to sell them—to Europeans.

Life began again when I met Basil Redless-Trench by the fish
display, where a dead shark lay prone on a bed of crushed ice. I'd
actually come there to pinch the ice from the display to chill a fizz-
less, half-finished can of Coca-Cola found earlier on the street. Now
it seemed something floated on the surface. Never mind, I had to act
fast. The guard who usually hovered over the food hall had left his
post, and I was digging under the shark's dorsal fin when I heard
Basil's smooth and knowing English voice.

"Stop before it's too late," he said. "You have alternatives."

"Too late," I screamed, as I slammed ice into can. Then I saw it
wasn't the guard but a genuine, tweedy, English aristo. I composed
myself. "I've tried every sales technique I've read of to persuade
Europeans to buy stocks and bonds from me. None has worked.
Europeans won't buy from Americans, because if they did, I could
afford to ship my ice maker from home."

Basil introduced himself. "All I meant is that there is a cold-water dispenser on the second floor. But I now see your problem runs more deeply than that. Perhaps your colonial sales techniques are the reason for your failure and present decrepit appearance."

What an absurd notion. I had lifted my salesmanship verbatim from the scribblings of American legends—Mark McCormack's "What They Don't Teach You at Harvard Business School," Peter Ueberroth's "Made in America," and Lee Iacocca's "Iacocca"— business wizards all. My actual sales skills I had bought long ago at a Dale Carnegie Seminar.

Dale Carnegie is an American model. In his day, the man toured the States with speeches called things like "How to Increase Your Profits Through Courtesy." His (profitable) magnum opus, *How To Win Friends and Influence People*, has inspired schools of influential pupils. It has been read by millions of people between New York and Los Angeles, and twice by everyone between Cleveland and Cincinnati where people are harder to persuade. Who could ignore patent truths like "courtesy will help you get ahead. Discourtesy is so rank and rife that the men and women who radiate courtesy are not going to have much trouble forging ahead."

Courtesy in Europe, however, had flopped, even when I radiated it. Selling things in Europe had been clouded by politics, language, and bloodlines, matters on which Dale Carnegie was silent. You try to win friends at an Arab bank after an American bombing of Libya. Worse, try explaining to an old Etonian how you really aren't certain of the identity of your maternal grandfather. Your high school French, even polished on Le Monde, will not tickle Frenchmen. *C'est dommage.*

"Look Basil," I said, weighing the choice between fishy Coke and fresh water two floors up, "There is no solution, Basil."

"The surname is not Basil," he said in the frigid tone I recognized as the response to my sales pitches. "You've been reading Dale Carnegie, and it is painfully obvious. I can tell by the way you try to be chummy with me, a man you've only just met, and insert my name repeatedly into an otherwise acceptable sentence."

He continued. "The most perverse behavior exhibited by you American salesmen derives from courses on how to win friends. It's as if you had skimmed Machiavelli's *The Prince*—you think you can manipulate people with such dimwitted codes of conduct. What else do you consider your sales techniques?"

I began to confess, a little at a time. I told him that Dale Carnegie taught me the six ways to win friends. Rule 3: "A man's name is to him the sweetest and most important sound in any language." That was why I had gone heavy on the Basils. I told Basil I never argued with a customer because the customer was always right, even when he was wrong. I told him I often asked questions of my customers not because I was curious, but because it made the customer feel good to appear knowledgeable (Rule 6).

Basil looked queasy, so I kept my other tricks well up my sleeve (Cardinal Rule) and followed Rule 2, "Be a good listener."

"Has anybody ever told you that you listen too much? To me you are harmless and painfully predictable. But to other Englishmen, you are warped. Dale Carnegie is not exportable."

"Take the concept of winning friends," he continued. "I don't even care to win my cricket matches, much less my friends. It's vulgar. Friends just happen to you over a three-hour lunch. Please, finish your confession so we can get to the core of your illness."

We weren't far away. To fit into Europe, I'd added what I thought of as a continental lacquer to my Dale Carnegie veneer. As usual, I'd gleaned the new me from a book, which began with a chapter called "Your nationality is a state of mind."

After that I began wearing ascots. I subscribed to *The Spectator* and bought two double-breasted suits. I should have known something was amiss when my father on his visit from home saw the suits and thereafter referred to me as "my son, the Euro-Wimp." But no, in a spasm of English conformity I learned to plant rosebushes. I began to pronounce "France," to rhyme with "prawns," instead of with "ants." Then I made ants, prañce, chance, lance, and almost every other word rhyme with prawns. And I don't even like prawns.

"There are three things you must do," Basil concluded. "First, purge yourself of whatever you read. Second, be American—it's your task. But most important, you must cease to think of yourself as a salesman. Deep down—I think—you are human. If you need to think of yourself as something, it does the least damage to be human. Neglect this lesson and you can kiss your platinum American Express card goodbye forever."

So I'm having a go at it. My biggest problem is finding books on the subject.

What the British
Can Learn from
American History

The invention of the telephone in 1876 gave the British a jolt from which they have never really recovered. The whole notion of a mechanism by which complete strangers can invade one's privacy is anathema to the British way of life. Deep down the British have always had it in for telephone callers, and so on Friday with the start of the Financial Services Act, the practice of young stockbrokers making unsolicited calls to people with money to invest—cold calling—will become illegal.

With this exception the Financial Services Act, known as the FSA, looks much like the American regulatory model, in spirit if not in every detail. Its *raison d'etre* is to protect private investors from shifty or stupid money men. Protection takes the form of a labyrinthine regulatory scheme in which several different police forces roam, at the top of which sits the British equivalent of the American Securities and Exchange Commission, called the Securities and Investments Board.

This is one instance where the British might have drawn lessons from American history. Some time ago I stumbled upon a charming and bright little book entitled *Fifty Years on Wall Street*, the memoirs of a securities salesman named Dean Matthey, who printed 101 copies of his thoughts in 1966 and gave them to his friends. In the book he recalls exactly what changed in America in 1933, and it is remarkably akin to what is changing in Britain in 1988.

"The Old English Common Law doctrine of caveat emptor—
'let the buyer beware'—was accepted in our colonies and established
in the main body of American law. Up to 1933 the buyer was supposed to be able to look out for himself. The seller was permitted to
tout his wares as long as he didn't blatantly misrepresent. Our heri-
tage was one of rugged individualists who could take it as well as
give it. However, not only Mr. Roosevelt but the people of this great
country, shocked by the excesses of the roaring twenties, for which
many groups were to blame, said 'This cannot happen again.' So we
changed from the concept of caveat emptor to the doctrine of caveat
vendor—'let the seller beware.' This fundamental change in our
basic thinking, in our mores, took place in but a few years."

The key difference between the births of the SEC and the Securities and Investments Board, known as the SIB, is that while the
American securities police force was conceived after the system had
collapsed and millions of small investors felt robbed of their savings,
the British laws were conceived in a boom, when no one had lost
anything but opportunity. The British financial markets were ticking along more or less honestly. With occasional nods and winks
from the Bank of England the cozy little oligarchy in the City had
policed itself well. Sure, there were problems that sullied the good
name of the City. But they either had nothing to do with the little
guy losing his savings, as in the crisis of Johnson Matthey Bankers.
Or they had little to do with the City, as when a manufacturing
company called Guinness manipulated its share price.

Why fix it if it isn't broken? I'll wager that the instinct to regulate has its origin partly in the vast increase in the number of small
shareholders in Mrs. Thatcher's Britain, but also in envy. City dealers have been too visibly prosperous. At the same time, consumer
protection groups have insisted there are two reasons why the small
buyer of shares, unit trusts, and insurance is far more exposed than
the buyer of, say, vacuum cleaners and needs special protection.
Small investors tend to be ignorant of what they're buying, and they
tend to commit a relatively large wad of money in any one transaction (rather like buyers of used cars, one might argue, except used
car dealers aren't getting rich)—fair enough. But the tendency of
those writing the new laws has been to assume that every conceiv-
able ripoff is worth preventing no matter what the cost. Therefore,

the cost of the FSA is going to be huge, far greater than the sum of the ripoffs that have happened to date in the City.

The known cost is £100 million a year direct levy on City firms. Much of this will no doubt be passed on to the little guy in the way of higher transactions costs. The rest will come from the pockets of City firms because, as the prices of their product will have risen, they will be selling less of it. The unknown cost, however, could be much greater than £100 million a year. For the Act introduces subtle but insidious inefficiencies into the financial markets.

I recently spoke with a man widely regarded as one of the most astute and scrupulous investors in London. He manages nearly £2 billion, some of which belongs to him. The Act essentially assumes that he is inclined to front run his clients—buy shares with his own money, then nudge the price with his clients' money. The Act therefore requires him to execute orders for his clients before he does anything for himself. He hasn't time for this. Often the markets are crazy, and he has not more than 30 seconds to buy or sell at a price. What he has always done is execute orders simultaneously and give his clients the best price. He will cope with the Act by simply excluding his clients from whatever quick decision he is making. Clients will effectively not get the full benefit of his wisdom. If I were a client I would be screaming for less protection.

This large money manager is further hobbled by the annoyingly detailed paper work he is required to complete. If his clients catch him breaking a single rule in the brand-new 213-page rule book, they will be able to claim damages that bear no relation to the injustice suffered. It could cost him a fortune. If, for example, he misclassifies a client as a "professional investor" who should really be a "business investor," the client can sue when an investment goes wrong. No one has bothered to make the punishment fit the crime under the Act. The astute money manager who previously spent his day making investment decisions will now pass his time vetting potentially litigious clients.

In the short, checkered history of American securities regulation, regulators have managed to produce millions of pieces of paper with lines of fine print for the public good, which no one can be persuaded to read. The Act, with its customer agreement letter, follows in this illustrious tradition. On Friday, the letter will be sent to, among others, the widows living on the south coast who control a substantial portion of the nation's savings. "They will drive their offspring mad with questions about this document," said a partner in a large City firm who is also an offspring. A more cynical person might conclude that these pieces of paper better protect regulators than they do small investors. Whatever the ultimate cause, the disease in British and American financial regulation is the same: no touch.

This wasn't supposed to happen here. First, the British have always had a clear sense of the principle of minimum supervision, which is why, for example, bobbies carry no guns. That shows a nice touch. Second, the SIB was supposed to attract "practitioners" with a feel for how the City worked. The watchdogs are paid roughly 175 percent of the going rate for equivalent civil servants just to soften the blow of leaving the City to become a regulator. Now there is plenty of fat in the City, plenty of old-timers made obsolete by Big Bang who can be enticed by a secure job as a regulator. But the reason they can be spared is that they were not particularly valuable practitioners. This isn't only my opinion; it is also the opinion of dozens of City workers with whom I have spoken. As a handful of City workers make the transition from second-rate practitioners to first-rate pains in the neck they are earning—over and above the 175 percent—the disdain of their former colleagues. A measure intended to smooth relations between the SIB and their charges has ironically backfired. The relationship between regulator and regulatee may come to be characterized by the same unhealthy mutual contempt that exists in America between Wall Street and the SEC.

The Act should have never departed from the principle of caveat emptor; the changes it introduced should have been more subtle, such as demanding more public information about brokers commissions. As it stands, the Act could open the floodgates to an amount of new, essentially meretricious, litigation. It runs the risk of shifting the focus of attention in the City from what is right and proper to what is merely legal.

Slicing Up Europe
for Fun and Profit

During the past few months*
Asher Edelman, Bruce Wasserstein, and Henry Kravis, among
other American heavyweights, have dedicated at least some of their
considerable brain cells to harassing corporate Europe. For the first
time in the 1980s there appears to be a dearth of American corporations worth looting. By far the most convincing evidence that our
leveraged takeover boom may be fizzling was Sir James Goldsmith's
announcement last March that he was packing up his hostile bidding
machine and flying it home—to England! Who ever moved from
America to England for money? Since Goldsmith had fed so generously at America's takeover trough, there was something vaguely
insulting in his decision to leave, like a dinner guest who really was
only after the free meal. Now that Sir James has made a $21 billion
hostile bid for the British conglomerate B.A.T., I for one would like
an explanation. Why doesn't he strip *our* assets? Is it something we
said?

Probably not. The same bittersweet scent that has driven
American investors wild with desire for the past five years is now
intoxicating the stock markets of Western Europe. One Brit in the
City of London describes it as "the odor of the American finan-
cier—a blend of sweaty ambition, jet fuel, and overpriced cologne."
This same man has pocketed tens of millions of dollars by simply

*This piece was written in October 1989.

guessing which company Americans and their proxies will target next. He held massive stakes, for example, in Gateway, B.A.T., and BTR before Wasserstein, Goldsmith, and Kravis made their moves. Recently he's taken positions in Germany and France, awaiting the arrival of the Masters of the Universe.

To use this man's real name would make him angry, and he's a composite anyway, a conglomeration of what the smart money in Europe is thinking these days. So let's identify him by what his wife might have screamed at their divorce proceedings: "that goddamn Ripper." That is what he is; that is what he does. He sits all day in a hard, wooden chair, cutting and slashing the balance sheets and income statements of European corporations with an enormous pair of scissors that he calls, without a trace of humor, "the Truth." Not that the Ripper terrifies, just the reverse. He is short. He lies about his height (five feet seven and a half inches). He stands on a book behind his desk when greeting visitors. He wears nerdy glasses and has bad teeth. He has, in short, the element of surprise on his side.

"I owe you a favor," said the Ripper as I entered his office, which looked like the captain's quarters on an elegant ship, "one favor. So I'll tell you about James Goldsmith. But if anyone finds out I'm your source, I'll let the Truth loose on your family jewels. We're playing hardball now." He snapped the blades of the Truth over his head, like a circus midget trying to prune a tall bush.

I tried not to smile. You know American culture has penetrated the U.K.'s financial markets when the biggest British players start making threats and using baseball metaphors. I looked down and noticed, beside his desk, a new pile of scraps on the floor.

"Just some things from B.A.T.," he said, watching my eyes.

A good place to begin: I told the Ripper I was confused. In particular, when Goldsmith—with Jacob Rothschild and Kerry Packer—announced his hostile bid for B.A.T., the one thing that was instantly clear was that he didn't have the money in hand, and he wasn't going to find it in England or anywhere else in Europe. The bid was announced as a complex swap of junk bonds and stub equity for B.A.T. shares among the three billionaires and British institutional investors. But this was laughable. British investors don't buy junk bonds. The money to buy the junk of B.A.T., Britain's third-largest company, would have to come from the only people on earth eager to swallow several billion dollars of risky bonds: Americans.

"That's true," he said. "That's why Jimmie hired Drexel and Bankers Trust to bankroll him. The bid is British in name only; the money and the spirit behind it are American."

Anyway, I said, since the bid was in essence American, British politicians had every right to squeal about the inability of their American counterparts to control their own money men. After the bid, I had expected to hear the same sort of embarrassed stammering from Washington as my neighbor makes whenever his pit bull squats in my front yard. You know: "Uh . . . sorry about that . . . hard to control the beast . . . I'd try to stop him, but it would only make him angry. . . ."

But something like the opposite was happening. With the conspicuous exception of the panicked chairman of B.A.T. (who called the billionaires "an ad hoc troupe of financiers"), most of the rude remarks have been made by Americans. More than two hundred senators and congressmen signed a letter asking Secretary of State James Baker to "communicate our concern to the British government." It went on in this sanctimonious vein: "Goldsmith and his financial supporters have served notice . . . that the use of debt to finance highly leveraged transactions has no limits."

What is more, the greatest threat to the bid was coming not from angry British politicians but from angry state politicians in America. B.A.T. owns the Farmers Group of insurance companies, and the insurance regulators of nine western states have served notice that in the interest of policyholders, they are determined to review rigorously the transfer of that asset to Goldsmith, Rothschild, and Packer, who have announced plans to sell Farmers to a French insurance company.

"Politicians everywhere," said the Ripper, "jump at the chance to grandstand for free, and American politicians have nothing to lose by alienating three foreign billionaires.

"Whatever happens in America, our government will *not* intercede to prevent leveraged takeovers and buyouts, partly because the toxic waste—the junk bonds—is going to be buried elsewhere, but also because Mrs. Thatcher has convictions about the free market that make George Bush look like a socialist. Maybe you noticed that Jimmie and Jacob lunched separately with Mrs. Thatcher *before* the bid. Those were not casual affairs. Those were reconnaissance missions. They now know exactly what she thinks. That is why they are so confident. That's one of the two reasons all of your sharks are swimming to Britain."

"What's the other?"

"Cheap companies—so cheap they make your teeth hurt. European stock markets are even less efficient than America's. Our analysts aren't as thorough, and our companies hide their assets: Makes them bloody hard to value—and to tax."

I said it didn't surprise me that any woman willing to incur the wrath of the electorate in order to privatize the water industry could rationalize hostile takeovers. I hadn't expected the British press to follow her lead, however. The three billionaires, and Goldsmith especially, are on their way to becoming heroes. B.A.T. (which in addition to its core tobacco business has bought completely unrelated enterprises like Farmers and Saks Fifth Avenue) has been mocked by the *Financial Times*, the *Telegraph*, the *Independent*, and the *Sunday Times* as a case study in how not to diversify. Why?

"Jimmie did two things right, and all of us who want to see more of this business owe him our gratitude. First, his target is the single best case in Britain for a hostile takeover. As Jacob has said, B.A.T. is nothing more than a machine for reducing capital values. Every dollar they touch turns to tobacco.

"Second, he didn't buy much of a stake in the company before he made his bid. He missed out on tens of millions of pounds of easy money. But he also completely avoided the charge of greenmail, which goes to show, by the way, that his motives aren't anything so innocent as money making. He longs to be worshiped—as the man who busted up the British conglomerates. Who knows why the press is playing along? The press works in mysterious ways, brainless lot."

I let that slide. "So you think Goldsmith will win?" I asked.

"*I did not say that!* I only said he *should* win. If I thought he'd win, I wouldn't have sold my shares on the day of the announcement. B.A.T. might be the best case for leveraged takeovers, but that doesn't mean it is the easiest to get. Farmers is, in effect, a poison pill. Anyway, there is only a tenuous relationship between the appropriateness of a target and the ease with which it is taken."

This led naturally to one of the two big questions I hoped to ask the Ripper. "What does that say about the LBOs that succeed? Are they good for society?"

"Please, spare the sentiment for my funeral."

"Okay," I said, moving to the second big question. "Then what about the future? What happens from here on, in Britain and on the Continent?"

With this, the Ripper picked up the Truth and went to a map of Europe on his wall. On this map were clusters of little flags, like pins on a golf course.

"When the Truth finds a target," he said, "I mark it for later."

The biggest cluster of pins was not in Britain but rather in Germany.

"Britain is the most likely because of the current political climate. On a six-month horizon, I'd have my money in British conglomerates and building materials companies, undervalued assets that are easy to strip.

"But Germany is potentially the most profitable. Germany is the virgin in the brothel. Its assets are veiled from the eyes of the pashas. Behind the veil, though . . . oh the charms, oh the charms . . . ahhhhh. . . ."

The Ripper for an instant seemed to have fallen into a suspended state of rapture.

"All you have to do," he said suddenly, "is to think back to the early deals in America, before anybody thought much about asset stripping and cash flow, to realize the pleasure to be had in Germany. Kluge made $3 billion on Metromedia in 1984. That's the sort of thing I expect from my German holdings in a few years."

PART III

OTHER WORLD

Twenty years ago it would have been strange for a young American without a special interest in Japan to do business with the Japanese. These days every young American I know seems to have had the experience. My own first exposure to Japan came six years ago, on the London trading floor of Salomon Brothers. When I first encountered the Japanese in the marketplace they had a well-earned reputation for being as reluctant as a nun on a date. Only after months of dinners, endless phone calls, and countless meetings over charts and graphs would they consider giving you business. There was always something cryptic in their methods. The phone would ring at your desk, and on the other end of the line would be

Mr. Yamamoto, whom you had seen off the previous night in a drunken haze, asking: "How now rong bond?" This was the Japanese way of asking for the price of thirty year U.S. government bonds.

"Ninety-six bid," you'd say.

"I buy $100 million," he'd say, then hang up—a friend for life.

By multiplying the transaction several thousand times, one could see how the finances of America and Japan were growing together. Every three months the U.S. Treasury announced its intention to borrow $10 billion or so, and every three months thousands of Americans looked at each other and asked the same question: "Will the Japanese buy?" Every three months a rumor circulated that the Japanese had lost interest in financing the American deficit. Every three months this rumor would cause the U.S. government bond market to collapse. Then the Japanese would start to buy—quickly. For when Japanese money moved, it moved all at once. Our conviction that it was being coordinated by some sinister force was only slightly weakened by the repeated, panicked calls from Mr. Yamamoto at Sumitomo asking if we'd heard what Mr. Tsujimoto at Mitsubishi was up to.

I couldn't help but grow curious. I wanted to know more about the unprecedented concentration of financial power in Tokyo. So the first thing I did upon quitting my job at Salomon Brothers was to find a magazine editor willing to send me to Japan. My excuse was the desire to research an article about what would happen to the world economy if Tokyo collapsed in an earthquake. The resulting piece, included here, ran on the cover of *Manhattan, Inc.* magazine, prompting a writer at the *Washington Post* to say that a New York magazine that devotes its cover to a Japanese earthquake must be starved for material. I'm willing to argue that the earthquake scenario was just a slightly crackpot way to ask a useful question: what would happen to us if the Japanese withdrew their savings from the world economy?

That question is being answered now, as Japanese bankers turn in on themselves to repair holes in their domestic finances caused by their own brand of financial madness. The net effect of the incredible disappearing Japanese has been to impose austerity on American borrowers and consumers. The new Japanese reluctance to throw money into all sorts of adventurous American financial schemes—from leveraged buyouts to small, new takeover firms—is also one of the main reasons the golden years on Wall Street have come to an end.

How a
Tokyo Earthquake
Could Devastate
Wall Street

In dusty libraries you can still find the odd copy of a fat black book published by the Japan Bureau of Social Affairs in 1926, a memento of the earthquake that leveled Tokyo at 11:58 A.M. on September 1, 1923, known as the Great Kanto Earthquake. Crackling descriptions of the physical trauma are punctuated by black-and-white photos of total destruction. The initial shock of roughly 7.9 on the Richter scale demolished every seismograph but one. It buckled railroad tracks into roller coasters and fissured the earth like a lady's nylon. The first, main shock was followed by two more shocks, then a quiver of 171 aftershocks. Within a few seconds, the tide raced out of Tokyo Bay and tidal waves raced back in, destroying the entire coastline. Within minutes, Tokyo itself was a chaos of bursting power lines, gas pipes, sewage channels, and water mains. Within hours, acres of buildings in the heart of the city had burned to ash.

All roads and communications were severed. Four hundred of the emperor's carrier pigeons—"gallant feathered messengers," the report calls them—were pressed into service (the emperor himself stayed out of town, discreetly insane). In the end, no one was safe, not even bankers. The stock market crashed, hundreds of banks failed, and the insurance industry was saved only by government intervention. And so it was that an act of God marked the end of Japan's first Economic Miracle (1867–1923), though they didn't call the era that back then and didn't realize it until later.

What is absent from the government's report is any remotely plausible sign of humanity. It tells of sixty thousand people who sought safety in the open ground of Hongo Park and were burned alive by a cyclone of fire that swept over them, of a city in ruins, of a population maimed, of treasures lost. Yet through it all the Japanese people stand silently stoic, like mannequins. Prince Regent Hirohito enters and exits the wreckage astride a horse, while straight-backed soldiers *in clean uniforms* salute crisply.

There is something vaguely unreal about the stiff upper lip of the Japanese people as scripted by the government's Department of Drama. I learned the extent of the fiction when I met in Tokyo an eighty-two-year-old man who had lived through the event. His mother was British and his father Japanese (a count, no less). In 1923 this man, then a sixteen-year-old boy, lived beside Tokyo Bay.

"You have no idea," he says. "When it hit, all you could do was crawl for safety, like an animal, a dog. Our house collapsed; then the tidal wave swept away the pieces. I watched this from my knees. The first thing you felt was anger, humiliation. Why does this happen to me? The Japanese felt it, I think, more than I. That's why they needed a scapegoat for the disaster. Thousands of Koreans were accused of arson and lynched. Westerners were let alone, but the word spread that the earthquake was no natural disaster, that a Western power had built an earthquake machine and aimed it at Tokyo. When the next one comes, I won't survive."

Neither may we. And that's what's harrowing about the thought of another great quake rocking Tokyo. The disaster of 1923 meant little outside Japan. Tokyo then occupied a tiny niche in the world economy. Tokyo now, were it a nation unto itself, would have a GNP of $730 billion, greater than Great Britain's. The entire labyrinthine Japanese government is in Tokyo. Twelve million people live in Tokyo narrowly defined. Thirty million Japanese live in the larger area that is the earthquake zone; 25 percent of the nation's population is vacuum-packed into the most treacherous 3.6 percent of the nation's land. Two-thirds of Japan's businesses worth more than 5 billion yen ($40 million) are headquartered in Tokyo. One-third of everything sold in Japan is sold in Tokyo.

The ports of Tokyo and neighboring Yokohama together export much of the chopsticks, computers, electrical appliances, ma-

chine tools, cameras, cars, and assorted gadgets that have created
Japan's $100 billion annual trade surplus. The mathematical conse-
quence of the trade surplus over the past decade are the hundreds of
billions of dollars, pounds, francs, and marks now controlled by
Japan's banks, insurance companies, and trust funds. These are all
headquartered in Tokyo. The branches of the world's eight largest
banks, which feed funds to the world, are completely dependent, in
an almost feudal way, on their head offices in Tokyo. Their cash
affects us all. In other words, the fate of the average foreigner is
intertwined with Tokyo's more than ever before, and more and
more every day. And, as we shall see, no foreigners are more exposed than Americans.

Whether or not the Japanese fully appreciate the degree to
which the rest of the world is implicated, they aren't oblivious of the
risks they run. The city's gas mains and bullet trains are neatly
programmed to cut off at the first whisper of seismic activity. Each
year the four prefectures in the earthquake zone—Tokyo, Chiba,
Saitama, and Kanagawa—hold mock-serious earthquake drills that
make everyone involved giggle. But it's hard to tell to what extent
the extra precautions taken by the Japanese government have offset
the incredible folly of situating the city most critical to the world
economy (name another if you disagree) atop a ticking bomb.

Earthquakes fall into two types: those that occur along the
boundaries of the earth's "plates"—mobile slabs of rock constantly
grinding against one another—and those that occur anywhere else.
The San Andreas Fault in California, for example, marks the border
of two plates. Earthquakes of the California variety are relatively
well understood. Geologists are at least willing to hazard guesses
about when interplate quakes might strike. Earthquakes that occur
away from plate borders—so-called intraplate quakes—are far more
mysterious. Tokyo lies over the intersection of four of the earth's
twelve or so major plates and so runs the highest risk in the world of
a California-style quake. But it is also plagued by the second, more
random, type of earthquake. The disaster of 1923 was of the second
type, one of an eerie pattern of massive intraplate quakes that have
devastated Tokyo roughly every seventy years going back nearly
four centuries: 1923, 1853, 1782, 1703, 1633.

"A catastrophic earthquake could happen any time," says

Kiyoo Mogi, head of Tokyo University's Earthquake Research In-
stitute. "I think the people don't know because there hasn't been a
big earthquake since 1923. People are accustomed to the resting
period."

The obvious response to Japan's earthquake problem would be
simply to move the Japanese government to another city. The Japanese discuss the subject frequently without, however, any real intention of taking action. Time and again on a reconaissance mission this
spring to Tokyo, I watched Japanese policy makers acknowledge
that the great quake might soon strike again, then wave a passive
hand at it. They seemed already to have decided that the concentration of power in Tokyo is necessary to manage Japan's aggressive
economic policy.

It is the single-minded pursuit of trade surpluses, coupled with
the belief that to generate surpluses the levers of power must remain
within the collective reach of bureaucrats, that has led to the crush-
ing concentration of economic life in Tokyo. In practice this means
that the Japanese government systematically rigs domestic prices to
give Japanese companies the strength to wage price wars overseas.
(It's no accident that Japanese goods are cheaper outside Japan than
in.) To fix prices at home, however, the bureaucrats require the
heads of the relevant companies, their shareholders, and their bankers to be close at hand. Ergo, Tokyo mushrooms.

Risking Japanese lives for the sake of global economic domi-
nation is not high on the list of subjects that the bureaucrats who
oversee the Japanese economy like to discuss with Western journalists. That, I think, is why I met with constant stonewalling in trying
to ask Japanese officials about earthquakes. When I suggested they
were avoiding me because they had no one versed on the subject,
they bridled. They said they had "earthquake plans." As long as
"plans had been made," it didn't seem to matter whether they were
the right plans or, indeed, even sensible. Not surprisingly, a lot of
them aren't.

Consider, for example, the relaxing of Tokyo's formerly strict
building codes, which, until 1981, restricted buildings higher than
sixty meters. Living, as I did, through even a tiny earthquake on the
thirty-first floor of a hotel focuses the mind wonderfully on construction standards. In the event, my hotel, the Imperial, rocked

back and forth; the man on night duty who answered my panicked call said that this was a good sign. Still, I wondered what would happen in a genuine disaster. I counted forty buildings with roofs higher than my hotel room. Japanese builders have responded to rocketing land prices by going higher and higher. I discovered that a lot of the skyscrapers in Tokyo have been built by the Kajima Corporation. I signed up for one of their press tours.

The tour began, appropriately, in the dark. The twenty or so Western journalists were shown a movie to excite us about Kajima. Aside from an eerie scene in which a thousand Kajima workers in yellow space suits throw up their hands and shout "Banzai!" the film was a succession of swaying skyscrapers. Buildings struck by earthquakes don't merely bounce up and down, as I had thought, but swing elliptically. The response to a shock from below is complex, and it only becomes more complex the bigger the quake.

When the lights flickered back on, six Kajima men stretched out along a table to face us, and the result was typical of what happens when Western journalists meet Japanese spokesmen. It reminded me of a tug of war on an ice rink. The Kajima men didn't speak English, and the journalists, for the most part, didn't speak Japanese. The head man kicked off. His words passed through a lady translator. American companies lagged far behind Kajima, he (or rather, she) said; Kajima was the leader in fifth-generation earthquake engineering, and so on.

A journalist had the gall to ask if there were any danger that a Kajima building might collapse in a big quake.

"All of the buildings of Kajima Corporation are earthquakeproof," said the head man, through the woman.

Another journalist raised her hand. "If the first-generation technology was earthquakeproof," she asked, "why bother with the new technologies?"

"He doesn't understand your question," said the translator and tried to move on.

But the American journalist persevered. "I still don't understand. . . . How can you say a building is completely earthquakeproof at the same time you are looking for technologies to improve its resistance to quakes? . . . How are the new technologies better? What was wrong with the old ones?"

At this, indulgent smiles broke out. "Yes," said the translator, "he agrees the new technologies are even better."

The technology in question is called an Active Mass Driver. It consists of sensors placed on each floor of a skyscraper to detect vibrations. They feed their data into a central computer. The computer keeps the building standing. This it does by throwing around weights to offset the shocks on each floor. The weights, in a sense, grapple with the earth. They move at 132 feet per second against the grain of a quake. I was inclined to believe that anything called an Active Mass Driver does whatever Kajima wants it to. After all, they were already using the technology in downtown Tokyo. But then they showed us how they had tested it.

The Active Mass Driver, it turned out, had never coped with anything greater than a medium-sized quake in simulations. It was confused by the complex shocks to a building from a massive earthquake. The system might mistakenly throw the weights in the *wrong* direction, adding to the effects of a really big quake. In view of this, Kajima decided to program the computer to turn itself off in the event of a major quake.

Moving from the buildings to their contents, consider the state of earthquake preparedness of the Tokyo Stock Exchange. The TSE computer is housed in a Tokyo neighborhood that was completely destroyed in 1923. I asked a panel of four TSE officials what would happen if their computer were lost in a major earthquake. "Ha," said the spokesman for the group, as if he had caught me flat-footed, "we have a backup computer."

"Where?" I asked.

"Next to the main computer."

Sure enough, as easy as it would be to store a spare copy of TSE records outside of Tokyo, there are *no* official records of ownership outside of that one building.

The political imperative of a centralized economy is clearly the reason Tokyo is allowed to grow and grow. But that doesn't fully explain the negligence I found. For *that* it's probably necessary to dig a bit deeper—till one strikes the strange (to us) Japanese attitude toward catastrophe. The idea of their city in ruins simply doesn't disturb Tokyoites the way it would New Yorkers, partly because it has happened so many times before, but also because the Japanese fully expect to rebuild. Some Japanese shrines, for example, are as a matter of policy destroyed and replaced every twenty years.

In her classic postwar study of Japanese society, *The Chrysanthemum and the Sword*, Ruth Benedict wrote, "No matter what the catastrophe, whether it was civilian bombing or defeat at Saipan or their failure to defend the Philippines, the Japanese line to their people was that this was foreknown and that there was therefore nothing to worry about. The radio went to great lengths, obviously counting on the reassurance it gave to the Japanese people to be told that they were living still in a thoroughly known world. . . . Japanese reassurances are based rather on a way of life that is planned and charted beforehand and where the greatest threat comes from the unforeseen."

The implicit corollary is that a catastrophe is acceptable as long as it can be said to have been foreseen. No problem there: *Everyone* in Tokyo knows there's going to be a big earthquake. It's only a matter of when.

The Japanese government's profound willingness to risk a holocaust is mixed with a (to Western eyes) shallower desire to maintain appearances. Several years ago, for example, the government passed an Earthquake Countermeasures Act. Under the Act, when geologists predict that the great quake is about to hit, committees of bureaucrats automatically meet to confront the impending disaster. But as yet, Japanese geologists refuse to make predictions, feeling that the small probability of being right doesn't justify repeatedly alarming the population.

However, I found a Japanese geologist willing to make a different sort of prediction. In December of 1988, sixty-five years after the last great Tokyo earthquake, a man in a Japanese ministry produced the government's first earthquake study. The picture it sketches is grim. And it has gone largely ignored within Japan.

The man in charge of the report is a young geologist at the National Land Agency named Hideaki Oda. We met in his makeshift conference room. Despite Tokyo's astronomical land prices, anyone within earshot of real power commands a room the size of a basketball court in which to host those famous consensus-building sessions. If you want to measure a Japanese man's clout, get him to show you his conference room. Oda had only a short black couch and a card table in the corner of his open-plan office. That office consisted of fifty or so metal desks piled high with papers, a hundred or so metal file cabinets upchucking more papers, and a few thousand square feet of linoleum littered with even more papers; the earthquake appeared already to have struck.

Oda spread out a series of maps of the city showing the effects of the next great quake, occurring at different times of the day and under different weather conditions. In each case, the greater Tokyo area was coated in dark red splotches (indicating damage) with the exception of a small circle of white. We were now sitting in that circle; it was the district that contains both the Japanese government and the Imperial Palace. These stand on a high rock about three miles from Tokyo Bay. Rock, Oda explained, is what you want to be standing on during a quake. He allowed himself a little giggle and said, "Only the government people will survive." That, he said, is why the government isn't worried.

Oda is not an alarmist. He just has an unusually good sense of humor. What is remarkable about his study is that it respects all of Japan's sacred cows—that the rock core of the city won't be much affected, that people will respond as humanely and efficiently as they do in government reports, that no important officials will perish, that skyscrapers will stand—and still it predicts Armageddon.

Many of Tokyo's citizens, like Holland's, live on unstable land that has been reclaimed from the sea. Neon signs are everywhere. So are bulk-chemical factories. Even if the skyscrapers don't fall, they've created new hazards by jamming people into perilously close quarters. And that brings us to Oda's central point: there are many dangers in Tokyo today that didn't exist in 1923. As one metaphor-friendly Japanese put it to me, Tokyo in 1923 was an abacus; today it is a supercomputer. It is dependent on automation and on sensitive technology. Bust an abacus, you can repair it in a day. Bust a supercomputer, it's broken for months. That will, of course, have an enormous effect on the world of money, which is completely dependent on high-tech communications. But on the subject of money, this Oda, like his government, is mute: "In the future we will discuss the problem of economic consequences."

That may not be necessary. Another Oda, Kaoru Oda, a young economist at the Tokai Bank in Nagoya, three hours south of Tokyo by bullet train, took the numbers from the National Land Agency and recently completed the first study of the global economic consequences of the next great Tokyo earthquake. I asked to see Oda's conference room, in order to place him on the nation's organization chart I was keeping in my head. It sat only four people comfortably. Why, I asked him, does a man with only a humble four-seater to his name make such bold (and risky) predictions? Well, he said after a pause, the Tokai Bank stands to gain if the Japanese capital is moved, because Nagoya is at the top of the list of places where it might move to. A second reason emerged later. This Oda, like the first, was genuinely enthralled by his subject. He was quirky, alive, and prone to idle speculation and imaginative drifting in a way Japanese businessmen and bureaucrats, who often seem to live in mortal fear of failure, seldom are.

The spadework of the Odas (cross-checked against the judgment of other experts) enables us to travel into the future. We can reflect on the Great Tokyo Earthquake of September 1, 1993, as if, in early 1994, a reporter had traveled around the world to compile a short history of the disaster and its financial consequences.

The first big shock of 7.9 on the richter scale struck Tokyo at 11:58 A.M., precisely seventy years after the earthquake of 1923. Tokyo's gas mains and bullet trains shut down, and its government offices stood, more or less, intact. But someone forgot to tell the people they were meant to be stoic.

Men working in the city wanted to know what had become of their families. First by car and then on foot, they raced out of central Tokyo. In an exclusive interview a senior official of the Ministry of Finance recalled, "I remember that, after the first blast shattered the glass, nothing stood between my ground-floor office and the open air. From beneath my desk (I was no hero) I watched a moving tangle of legs: men running; men falling; men bleeding; men fighting."

From the air, Tokyo looked like an angry ant colony, stepped on, then ignited. One hundred fifty-two thousand people were killed, mostly by fire—about six times the number killed in Armenia in 1988. Black humor has it that Japanese earthquakes discriminate against the poor (whose houses suffered most) but that fires are brutally egalitarian (several leaders of Japan's ruling Liberal Democratic

Party and at least two bank presidents are known to have perished by fire). Two hundred five thousand people were injured. Most survivors were homeless. What is remarkable is that the numbers were precisely those predicted by Hideaki Oda of the National Land Agency, who has come to be seen as a kind of prophet.

By noon, two minutes after the first shock, eight hundred thousand buildings (10 percent of the total) had collapsed. A phenomenon unique to earthquakes called liquefaction, in which soft ground turns to Jell-O, jostled 41 percent of the soil near Tokyo Bay. Several chemical factories in the area exploded. It is now agreed that is where many of the fires began.

Most men worked in glass and steel. But they lived, as ever, in wood. Of Tokyo's 8.5 million structures, 7.25 million were wooden. Of these, 2.57 million burned to the ground; 3.75 million were badly damaged. The fires burned for days, until they ran out of fuel. The ability to fight them was all but lost. Fire trucks got stuck in fissures or behind walls of automobiles. Japanese leaders have claimed car accidents were the sole reason for serious fire damage, but this is seen by Western observers as a spurious rationalization by politicians who wish to rebuild the capital in Tokyo. The truth is Tokyo has always been blocked solid with traffic.

The greatest irony of the event, in retrospect, was that the last thing anyone thought about on September 1 was money. Throughout that first day Western politicians voiced their sympathy. Everyone agreed that earthquakes were a bad thing. Not everyone could agree, however, on what to do when they occurred in a rich country like Japan. Gorbachev merely sent condolences, the idea of the Soviet Union giving economic aid to Japan being simply too ludicrous. The United States shipped emergency supplies of rice, among the first American rice ever allowed on Japanese soil. As ports and roads no longer existed, the rice was airlifted from the ships by helicopter.

The shortage of reliable news has been given as the reason for the indecisive Western response to the event. All the journalists on the Pacific Rim chartered boats to take them to Tokyo, only to find when they arrived that they needed boats to ship their copy out. More than a third of Tokyo's telephones and almost half of its electricity hubs were wiped out. The Tokyo telephone network closed for a month and did not fully recover for nearly four months. The prodigious Hideaki Oda had foreseen this as well, basing his forecast on a single incident. In November 1984 a fire swept through the communications cables in Tokyo's Setiyama ward. It took eight days for normal phone service to be restored. This time there was damage not only to the entire system but to the repairmen and to their company. As a result, the Great Tokyo Earthquake of 1993 is a case study of the enormous consequences of lacking information in the information age.

This loss alone would have been enough to close Tokyo's financial markets. But the Japanese suffered another setback. The official records of share ownership vanished. No one had a clue who owned what. Half of the world's stock market capitalization trades on the Tokyo Stock Exchange (compared to 25 percent in New York). Despite its size, the market in Japan has been quaintly primitive. Computers play a much smaller role there than in New York. Shares are pieces of paper physically delivered by the seller to the buyer three days after a transaction. Until delivery, the official records of ownership are (or were) blips in the main computer of the TSE, an antiquated Hitachi. The machine, and hence billions of dollars of Japanese stocks, stood in a building near Nihonbashi, an area gutted by fire. Several vaults holding the shares themselves, also in Nihonbashi, were lost as well.

During the crash of October 1987, the New York Stock Exchange computer lost a file of records. New York, however, had a genuine backup. The slips that the NYSE computer automatically sends to brokers became Black Monday's official records. The Japanese lacked adequate technology because the Ministry of International Trade and Industry (MITI) had forbidden the Tokyo Stock Exchange to buy an American computer, and American computers are the only ones that do the job properly. Black Friday, as the day of the quake is now called, was a bleak one for Hitachi's public relations department. In short, because of Japan's economic policies, the TSE was in complete disarray. The confusion, coupled with the communications failure, provided the Ministry of Finance with an airtight alibi for closing Japan's stock markets. Oddly enough, though for different reasons, this too had been predicted in late 1988, by Kaoru Oda of Nagoya's Tokai Bank.

In the canyons of Wall Street, the back alleys of the City of

London, and other financial centers, many people shook their heads and said how sad it was. But only poor people and poets gave the human loss their undivided attention. Rich men's emotions were fully invested in their portfolios. If you owned shares in Japanese companies, your first reaction was to sell them. But where? When the quake struck it was 11 P.M. on Thursday in New York. Traders and investors received news of it on their home televisions. There was nothing for them to do but wait until the London markets opened five hours later.

Nothing jolts the City of London out of its sleepy mornings and long lunches like a good disaster in the middle of the night. The City then makes all those decisions that would normally be made hours later in Manhattan but that all of a sudden cannot wait. By 7 A.M. on Friday, September 1, fantastic volumes of yen and Japanese shares were changing hands in London. Buyers quickly lost their appetites, however. The only strong sector seemed to be construction stocks; shares in a construction company called Kajima soared. The yen and other Japanese shares were sinking fast.

Western speculators, having sold short Japan's shares and currency, wanted to be reassured. By noon (by which time all of Wall Street was on the phone) they were frantic. They craved information. Had Sony's headquarters survived? How about its famous chairman? What was Sony's new value? But since news leaked out of Tokyo slower than ketchup from a bottle, estimating damages was impossible. There was only one place to turn: the Tokai Bank report of December 1988. The report was hungrily faxed about Wall Street and elsewhere and assumed to be the next-best thing to being in Tokyo. The report explained how the loss to Japan's capital stock would come to 80 trillion yen ($670 billion) and that the replacement cost would be 119 trillion yen ($991 billion). These were not bad guesses. The actual loss seems to have been the equivalent of $1.3 trillion.

Upon reading the Tokai Bank report, there was, in retrospect, one question that every foreign-exchange trader, every bond trader, every equity trader, and indeed anyone with money to invest, should have asked. From where would the more than $1 trillion to repair Tokyo come?

The economic world is a web; subtract one filament and the

whole is weakened. Along with the yen, shares of most Western insurance companies collapsed. American International Group, for example, one of the largest insurance holding companies, was down 25 percent, with no buyers in sight. Japanese bureaucrats had seen to it that Japanese fire-and-earthquake insurance migrated overseas: to Australia, to Lloyds in London, to New York. Foreign insurance companies had been delighted to suck up as much Japanese risk as they could. Japan was seen as a prudent, orderly, risk-averse society. Insurers forgot that, though the Japanese were loath to take small risks, they had embraced the biggest risk of all.

On Saturday there was the inevitable speculation that the group of seven (minus Japan, of course) would temporarily close world stock markets. The lead story of Sunday's *New York Times,* however, laid that theory to rest. It contained the following words from U.S. Treasury Secretary Nicholas Brady: "The lesson of the crash of 1987 is not that markets should be closed in times of crisis. Closing stock markets causes more problems—by feeding panic and so on—than it solves. The lesson of the crash of 1987 is that a few investment firms, by program trading, can create undesirable distortions in the stock market. This administration has spoken with the heads of the larger firms that still engage in program trading, and we have agreed that they will suspend their activities."

On Monday, September 4, the stock markets collapsed. It happened as follows. Western insurance companies made public their exposure to Japan. The numbers exceeded market expectations by tens of billions of dollars. Insurance shares, of course, fell further. But they dragged others with them. The insurance companies hadn't nearly enough money invested in Japan to cover their losses. They were forced to liquidate their holdings of American, British, French, German, Italian, and Australian stocks and bonds. The very thought drove the markets down. Speculators piled in, selling short in anticipation of the event. Panicky investors and strapped arbitrageurs sold, too. In fact, the Dow Jones Industrial Average nosedived 220 points even before insurance companies began selling.

Meanwhile, the silence from Japan was deafening. Day after day the biggest news was that no Japanese had bought or sold. Up to September 1993, the Japanese had left footprints in the markets, but one never actually saw them. One surmised that they had been buy-

ing U.S. Treasury bonds because the U.S. Treasury-bond market
had leapt. But one never actually *knew*. On September 15, all this
changed. The first Japanese twitch came in New York. Salomon
Brothers, Goldman Sachs, and other brokerage firms were inun-
dated with calls from senior Japanese bankers and brokers, all asking
frightening questions: "Please, could you give me your bid on $1
billion worth of Treasury bonds? Please, could you give me your bid
on 3 million shares of General Motors? Please could. . . . " When the
Japanese finally emerged, flexing aching muscles, the world
changed forever: They wanted their money back!

Not surprisingly, they have been blamed for neglecting our
interests. But Japan's minister of finance had a point when he wondered aloud whether the West would have shown Japan any greater
consideration were the shoe on the other foot. If 30 million Americans wanted to withdraw their savings from the bank to replace
their homes and chattels, would our politicians have had the will to
refuse? No Japanese government could deny its people their wealth.
Before the disaster Japan's bankers had agreed among themselves
that if ever a truly massive quake hit, a limit of one hundred thousand yen per person in deposit withdrawals would be imposed. But
that was merely to tide them over until the Bank of Japan reopened
and injected funds. This it did on September 15.

On that day, all became clear or, rather, confused in a new way.
The $1.3 trillion the Japanese required to rebuild Tokyo was to
come mainly from New York and London. From their point of
view, foreign liquid assets were slack, their national nest egg. The
rest of the world, however, depended on them. And from September 15, 1993, the price of everything in the world that could be
traded quickly—stocks, bonds, currencies, commodities—was
driven by this single enormous movement of Japanese assets. Ten
years of chits were called in at once.

The banks weren't the only channel through which Japanese
money came home to roost. Japanese life-insurance companies
helped, too. They held something like $200 billion of foreign invest-
ments. By law the life-insurance companies were not required to
pay on deaths caused by earthquakes. But in Japan the law often
comes second—in 1923 the insurance companies were ordered to
pay money they didn't owe. In a crisis no Japanese company is

really private; the insurance companies have been effectively nation-
alized. They have been told to pay whatever they can without de-
pleting their domestic-securities portfolios. It is their peculiar charm
that they don't argue.

The world stock markets (except, of course, for Japan's, which
was closed) went into a free-fall. But this crash looked nothing like
October 1987. It was worse. To the Federal Reserve, the sudden
absence of Japanese money resembled a minicollapse of the banking
system; our biggest lenders simply disappeared. To the collapse of
the stock market was added the collapse of the bond market, which
meant that interest rates rose dramatically. Japan was selling her
foreign shares. Japan was selling her U.S. Treasury bonds. Japan
was selling her platinum. Japan was bidding up the price of oil. All
the seemingly hysterical reports were true. But what was more important, in retrospect, was what Japan was not doing.

At the end of 1986 Japanese banks had $1.02 trillion in out-
standing loans to foreign countries. In 1989, eleven Japanese banks
together had lent roughly half of the $25 billion used by Henry
Kravis to buy RJR Nabisco. For a week after the great quake, Japanese banks worldwide, lacking instructions from Tokyo, were para-
lyzed. They ceased to lend altogether. The banks revived when
communications with their head offices were restored, but by the
end of 1993 Japan's Ministry of Finance was said to have a "no-loan
policy" toward Western companies. Japan has ceased to supply
funds to Henry Kravis, and Henry Kravis has ceased to make leveraged buyouts.

In 1987 New York City developers had feared that a glut of
fifteen thousand new condominiums would depress real estate
prices. That fear proved groundless only because Japanese buyers
mopped up the surplus. After last September, Japan ceased to buy
Western property. They had always paid with money borrowed
from Japanese banks against inflated Tokyo real estate. The higher
the value of real estate in Tokyo, the more big Japanese real estate
companies could borrow to buy high rises in Manhattan. A single
Japanese company, Mitsubishi Estate, owned outright $300 billion
worth of land in downtown Tokyo. It could, in theory, have borrowed against the land to buy most of London. The Japanese were,
therefore, the plug in the international real estate market. The earth-

quake pulled the plug. When the value of Tokyo land crashed and the Ministry of Finance insisted that bank loans go only for domestic rebuilding, the Japanese banks ceased to indulge Japanese buyers of foreign real estate.

On September 23, the Bank of Japan further announced that, to encourage rebuilding, Japanese people and firms would be permitted loans at 1 percent interest. Japanese optimistically queued to retrieve money that represented not only their past surpluses but future ones too. The money appears to be rebuilding Tokyo in better condition than it was before. Toyota, for example, although it has plenty of cash of its own, borrowed to build a new plant to meet the brisk domestic demand for its cars.

IMPORT NOW, said the push carts at Tokyo's Narita airport (in English) before they melted in the fires. Since the earthquake, Japan's bureaucrats have ceased this sort of crafty posturing, not because they've found religion, but because it's no longer necessary. They have no choice but to buy imports. Overnight they have become a nation of consumers—the disaster has spurred fantastic demand, especially for housing and factory equipment. (The Tokai Bank's Oda had predicted that Japan's postquake growth rate would be 12 percent in 1994 and 10 percent in 1995.)

What is more, the Japanese export machine has spluttered. Toyotas, Sony Walkmen, VCRs, and Camcorders are flowing again from Japan, but not in the same quantities as before, partly because production lines have been severed, partly because the Yokohama and Toyko ports were half-swallowed by tidal waves, partly because many workers were killed, and partly because 30 million surviving Tokyoites want new autos and VCRs for themselves. General Motors, Phillips, and other companies that make near substitutes for Japanese goods are beginning once again to dominate their home markets. Oda had predicted that Japan would run a trade deficit for the next five years, and the evidence thus far is that he was right. From a surplus of $85 billion in 1987, Japan will fall into an annual deficit as great as $11 billion—leaving no spare funds to invest in U.S. Treasury bonds.

The sudden scarcity of money abroad has been the most dramatic effect of the destruction of Tokyo. In Washington, the chairman of the Fed, Alan Greenspan, lay awake in his bed until the wee hours each September morning. He occasionally padded to the fridge for a glass of milk to settle his stomach. If he had read the Tokai Bank report, he would have seen that Oda had forecast a big rise in U.S. and European interest rates and had predicted that rates would remain high for three years after the quake. Following the disaster (which to central bankers was not the earthquake but the withdrawal of Japanese money from their respective countries), the entire West faced the same problem, only Greenspan's was extreme. America depended far more heavily on Japan than did Europe.

Inflating the money supply doesn't come naturally to Alan Greenspan, who is almost phobic about inflation. He has apparently decided to ignore the very real danger of depression and simply let nature take its course. The small amounts of money he has injected into the banking system have had no effect on the credibility of Oda in Tokyo. As Oda foresaw, interest rates have risen by 5 percent.

Five percent: the number is more evil than many suppose. Anyone in debt is in trouble. The landscape will soon be littered with unfinished or foreclosed houses. Japan's construction industry is thriving; ours is crippled. America's already destitute savings-and-loan industry, which holds hundreds of billions of dollars of long-term home mortgages financed by short-term borrowings, looks as naked as a tall Texan in a shrinking suit. The lots of small-town car dealerships are filled with unsold American autos because no one can afford a loan to buy one. Detroit may have won back from the Japanese a bigger share of the American market, but that market is suddenly much smaller.

As the West's leading financial city, New York has suffered by far the most from the earthquake. Water fills the deep holes from which skyscrapers were to have risen. Cobwebs fill unsold condominiums. Despair floods the minds of unemployed beeper manufacturers, Rolex watch salesmen, and society florists. Tables are empty in restaurants as are seats on Broadway. The aftershocks have been felt at every level of Manhattan society. William Everage, a forty-one-year-old shoeshine man on Wall Street, sees it this way: "I was doing 125 wing tips a day before Black Monday. I was doing 90 before the earthquake. Now, on a good day, I do 50, and the customers aren't so friendly anymore. The wife and I wanted to take out a loan to buy the new Ford. They went and raised the price of the loan. It seems like the price of everything has gone up except houses. They've gone down."

In Washington the most popular political defense has been to redirect criticism toward the Japanese. The more responsible media have seen through this line. "Live by the Yen, Die by the Yen" was the headline of a recent editorial in *The New York Times* that argued that, since successive conservative administrations had been both causal agents and benefactors of the unprecedented expansion of consumer credit, they should suffer when our debts become too onerous to bear.

Subscribers to the *Wall Street Journal* knew the cruelest irony of all. On October 1, 1993, one month after the holocaust, with money pouring back into Japan, the Tokyo Stock Exchange re-opened. The wiping out of more than $1 trillion in assets would have sent most stock markets crashing. But the fate of the Japanese market is not so mundanely decided. It is determined by the flow of money into the market from large Japanese institutions, which in turn is determined by the Ministry of Finance. And that has led to the strangest irony of the disaster: upon reopening, the Tokyo Stock Exchange rose.

What happened was no different from what often occurs in Japan, only a more extreme case. Stocks were "ramped." To ramp a stock, brokers conspire to buy it all. A Nomura broker whispers in his client's ear to buy the stock of Company X. Then Nomura spreads a happy rumor about Company X: Company X is soon to be awarded a big government contract! Nomura buys the stock with the money of its other clients. The stock jumps 10 percent in a day. When the market sees the ramp and hears the rumor, all join in. Someone eventually is left holding the bag, but not Nomura. What the Ministry of Finance did after the earthquake was, in effect, to ramp the entire stock market. It was only a matter of sending out a few carrier pigeons from the ministry's windows to the big Japanese banks, insurance companies, and money funds. Japan, in effect, took itself private, which is what a lot of companies do when the public undervalues them.

And where did the money come from to buy up the shares? Easy, it came from America and from Britain and from France and from Australia—everywhere but Japan. Two-thirds of Japan's foreign reserves had returned to answer real needs. The rest came home to answer financial needs. And the mystery of the ramping of the TSE today is that it's still going up; i.e., no one seems to have been left holding the bag. Or at least that is what the Ministry of Finance will tell you. We in the West might disagree.

The Tokai Bank report on the economic consequences of the next huge earthquake is no more than a collection of very educated guesses. It neglects many issues; in particular it does not dwell for long on the microeffects within the real economy. Will companies outside Tokyo leapfrog companies in Tokyo? Oda also didn't bother to consider the political consequences of a massive withdrawal of Japanese capital. Will Japan bashers be elected in the West? Will the safety of Tokyo, in the future, be regarded as too important to be left to the Japanese? Will the end of prosperity signal the end of the West's political drift rightward in the 1980s? Will Tom Wolfe label the new young poor of the 1990s "tremor babies"?

The narrow message from Oda is that the financial consequences of a Tokyo earthquake will be felt primarily outside Japan. It will deal no fundamental blow to the prosperity of Japan. The wealth of the nation, it is assumed, is in the structure of its society. And the nation will recover quickly. As far out as 1998, however, the United States will continue to suffer from a yearly decline of 2.7 percent in the growth rate of its real GNP; the European Community's annual decline will be .3 percent; Latin America's, 13.6 percent.

The broader lesson is that the imbalances in the world's financial markets are a disaster waiting to happen. Today, when foreign journalists stumble into MITI and demand to know what will be done about Japan's trade surpluses, they sometimes get this strange answer: "When the earthquake comes, the trade surplus will go away." The good news from Oda is that it's probably true. The bad news is that we'll wish it wasn't.

The New York
Investment Banker
Abroad

Nothing can remain in Tokyo for long without being fitted into the city's many-storied status structure. Tokyoites rank everything—baby clothes, buildings, novelists, mountains, department stores—with such cold-blooded precision that they sometimes seem to be acting out a parody of the Sutton Place view of the world. The difference is that the constant struggle between snobs and reverse snobs that keeps New York society in check (the moment something is *in* for some, it is *out* for others) doesn't exist in Tokyo; in Tokyo there are only snobs. Ask any six Japanese to rank the hotels of Tokyo, for example, and you'll receive six identical lists. Second on that list is the Imperial, the choice of Dutch bankers and middle American manufacturing executives. First is the Okura, where Sony Chairman Akio Morita roams the halls in the middle of the day and Prime Minister Kaifu takes his saunas. The Okura is also where you can find the investment bankers from New York.

I'm told that it didn't take long for the boys to work out where to sleep in the world's most status-conscious city. On a rainy morning this spring I found them milling in the gentle gloom of the Okura lobby. By ducking into a nooky corner and remaining completely silent, I was able to spot more New York investment bankers than I've seen since I left my job at Salomon Brothers: Pete Peterson, a brace of Goldman Sachs associates, and a lesser managing director of Salomon Brothers. (I later learned I had missed John

Gutfreund by only a few hours.) For five glorious minutes I hid behind a pillar and watched quietly as Joe Perella flipped idly through a copy of *Time* magazine. It occurred to me that the only thing more ridiculous than traveling seven thousand miles to read *Time* was traveling seven thousand miles to watch someone else read *Time*.

On second thought, it was worth every mile. A city in which I was a complete stranger became at that moment more familiar than most places in America. On each of my subsequent visits the Okura was infested with recognizable American financial types, and it was hard, when there, to avoid sentimental pangs of patriotism.

Sometimes they stood outside on the sidewalk with horror on their faces, as wolf packs of Japanese schoolboys in yellow hats wandered by them shouting Hello! Hello!, or *Haro! Haro!*, which appears to be the more usual pronunciation of the Japanese. Once I saw an especially forlorn banker who had bought himself a plastic cup of yogurt. He wasn't eating it. He was staring incredulously at the prose on its side, which only a Japanese manufacturer could write: *In the lust generation, any women like to taste the sweet meat as it melts and beat to the beat of her hot heart. These are the taste as first love which we cannot forget.* He forced a smile. I like to imagine he was reminding himself why the hell he'd left home to stand on a Tokyo street corner reading the side of a yogurt cup: "I, Martin Saxon III, from Marblehead, Massachusetts, and the Wharton School, am an *international businessman.* "

But most of the bankers simply planted themselves in the Okura's airport-cocktail-lounge-style chairs, summoning the energy to strike out once again and preach the gospel according to Wall Street to heathen Japanese investors. The American financier might prefer to think of himself as Commodore Matthew Perry sailing his black ships boldly into Edo Bay in 1853. But his true progenitors are the Dutch and Portuguese who landed here more gingerly in the mid-sixteenth century to peddle Chinese silks and the Jesuits' brand of Christianity. A deal was struck. In exchange for flirting with the new religion, the Japanese were given guns and other neat European toys. It's clear who got the long end of that bargain: Fifty years after the barbarian missionaries arrived, they were expelled, and the Dutch traders were confined to a tiny island off the coast of

Nagasaki. The Japanese who had converted and refused to renounce their new faith were massacred with a flair that would have impressed Torquemada.

The challenge for American financiers is pretty much the same as it was for the Jesuits, with adjustments for a few hundred years' progress in human rights. The cult of the financier simply doesn't have the following in Japan that it has in America. Japanese investment bankers more closely resemble American investment bankers of the fifties than those of today; they are the handmaidens of industry rather than the vehicles with which to torment industry. Japanese bankers don't put companies "in play," don't refer to themselves as Big Swinging Dicks, and don't get their pictures on the covers of glossy business magazines.

Their equity analysts refuse to recommend the sale of a company's stock, for fear of angering its management. When they aren't kowtowing to their corporate clients they are sucking up to the Ministry of Finance (MOF). The MOF bosses the bankers in ways unimaginable in government-wary America. When the MOF tells Nomura to buy stocks to stop the market tumbling, for example, it actually does it.

The problem is fundamental: to the Japanese the investment banker is a middleman, and they have long viewed middlemen as pimps. As improbable, as outrageous, as unthinkable as it seems, investment bankers and whores are probably nearer to each other in the Japanese status structure than the Okura and the Imperial. This lack of respect for Wall Street's finest has led to some great moments in international relations. One American investment banker, for example, recalls a meeting with a group from a major Japanese real estate company. The Japanese sat along one side of the conference room while one of the Americans, speaking English and using slides, pitched a piece of Manhattan real estate. Right in the middle of the show, the chairman of the Japanese real estate company picked up and left. His minions split quickly into small groups and began to jabber (in Japanese, of course), oblivious to the American still making his presentation. In the midst of the confusion one of the Japanese points to the investment banker and says in Japanese, "Never mind him. He's only the whore's pimp. All he wants is money. There's no need to listen to the whore's pimp. . . ."

Now imagine the shock of Martin Saxon III when he hears he is a pimp. Say he is dining with a new Japanese client. How does he convey to a man he has only just met that he is widely known by those who count in America as a Big Swinging Dick? That in America he is the human equivalent of the Okura Hotel? He can, of course, open the meeting in the stylish and forceful manner of the Drexel trader visiting a large Japanese client who delivered the memorable line: "You little shit, don't you ever talk that way to me again." But I am told by an American who sells bonds to Japanese that there is a more effective way: brag and drop every name you can think of.

So Martin Saxon III looks around the restaurant to make sure no one he knows from back home is listening. Then he grits his teeth and says, "You probably didn't know that I graduated first in my class from Wharton and was voted by my classmates as the person most likely to be the next Donald Trump. My father knows George Bush." Maybe he pulls from his briefcase the back issue of *Business Week* that carries his photograph. And, lo and behold, it works—sort of. The client nods and sucks wind through his teeth and begins to treat him nicely. For the first time since he arrived Martin Saxon feels a little surge of . . .

Hope. That's what keeps Saxon from fleeing the degradation on the first flight out of Tokyo. He learns that the Japanese are suckers for American status symbols. He gives them what they want, and he begins to get respect. He might even start stretching it a bit: "My father plays golf with George Bush." As he builds a rapport with a few gray-haired Japanese executives, he begins to dream of pulling the Golden Lever. The Golden Lever, the crank handle on the side of the Matterhorn of cash that rises high in central Tokyo, becomes the key to Martin's happiness. Pull the lever, he imagines, and a panel on the side of the alp slides open, and a black-haired man in a blue suit comes scurrying out with a rickshaw full of money that he dumps at your feet and says, "Buy me Rockefeller Center and keep the change," or some such outrageous thing. The World Trade Center, IBM, California, Hungary—you can never tell what he'd like to buy next. All you know is that the bigger his purchase, the better he tips.

And the depths of his pockets have yet to be plumbed: In a

two-hour stroll through Tokyo you can brush past more treasure than has ever been hoarded in so small a space in the history of man. Between Shinjuku to the west and Marunouchi to the east are crammed most of the assets of the Pacific Rim. Never mind the rest of Japan. The purchasing power in Tokyo alone is essentially unlimited.

There are probably hundreds of men here who could outbid the Getty for a van Gogh. When I asked a Japanese friend who works in real estate how many millionaires he thought there were in Tokyo, he shook his head and said, "Everyone, maybe," and saw nothing unusual in the idea. I've met a proprietress of a Ginza hostess bar who is looking for big chunks of real estate on Cape Cod. I know a noodle shop owner who buys leveraged leases on Boeing 747 jets as tax shelters. The financially ambitious New Yorker stares at the buildings and knows two things with certainty: that they are full of money and that he can't get inside to touch the stuff.

Of course as every investment banker knows, there are a few American financial success stories in Tokyo. A trader at Salomon Brothers has for the last three years taken about $100 million a year out of Tokyo for his firm. Pete Peterson and the Blackstone Group were paid $100 million by Nikko Securities for 20 percent of their company. Joe Perella had $100 million dumped in his lap by Nomura in exchange for 20 percent of *his* company. But by and large everyone agrees that compared to the mountain of money, $100 million is a pimple. Even the Japanese investment bankers make more than that. Last year Nomura raked in $3 billion in pretax profits. No, these chunks of $100 million are flukey small change. Still, they cause otherwise sensible men to neglect the remarkably simple history of the Western prospector in Japan: he comes, he feels welcomed, he sees big money on the horizon, he tells the Japanese his deepest secrets; he sees big money before his eyes, and then . . . it vanishes—poof.

Because there's so much commotion on the surface of Tokyo, it's easy to forget that no one like Joe Perella has ever controlled anything meaningful in Japan. Americans get permits to open branches in Japan. Americans get licenses to sell their products in Japan—for example Merrill Lynch will be allowed to introduce money market funds. American firms are growing—the offices of

Morgan Stanley, Salomon Brothers, First Boston, Shearson Lehman, and Goldman Sachs have all about doubled in the last two years. But Americans, unlike their Japanese counterparts, are not making money; with the exception of Salomon Brothers, I haven't been able to find any American firm in a position to brag about its performance in Tokyo. The other firms have assumed the missionary position, which is to say they are flat on their backs looking skyward to God for help.

They are, however, making a few converts. The Japanese who populate the Tokyo offices of Wall Street firms are strange hybrids of East and West. Their uneasiness is manifest in the Japanese-style employee broadcast sheets that circulate in American firms at the end of each recruiting season. The sheets hold a few paragraphs written by each of the new Japanese employees, designed to show how happy they are to come to work at Shearson Lehman or First Boston. These days the statements circulate only in Japanese. As one Shearson banker said, "We stopped translating them into English because they'd say things like 'My name is Watanabe, and all my friends and family advised me not to work for an American company. I don't know why I did, but in spite of my fears I am hoping for the best.'"

The converts are an indication of how hard the Wall Streeters are trying; you couldn't blame them for not trying. They probably deserve to realize at least the modest ambition of providing conventional financial services to the Japanese. In the last ten years America has built truly awesome financial machines staffed by some of the best brains money can buy. They know more ways than ever to separate investors from their money—some of which are even beneficial to the investors. Certainly they know more than Japanese financiers, who have lived a singularly cozy and protected life.

Until about five years ago no one in Japan seriously thought of investment banking as an international business; it was strictly a domestic cartel. The market share of the Big Four—Nomura, Nikko, Daiwa, and Yamaichi—is effectively stabilized by the Ministry of Finance. So are the profits: commissions on Japanese stocks and bonds are fixed ten times higher than in America. You'd be pressed to find an industry sleepier than Japanese investment banking. The Japanese may have excelled in manufacturing high technology but they've been awfully slow to use it, and the money of this world is being run more and more by computers. A former employee of Yamaichi says that despite repeated requests, he was never in his three years on the job granted permission to use a personal computer. A French investor who visited Nomura and asked for a historical chart of prices of Japanese government bonds was greeted by a man with a shopping cart full of hand-kept records (any American broker could pull this sort of thing up on a screen in a few seconds). And even when they do incorporate machines, Japanese financial people seem mystified by what they do. A Nikko Securities commercial for a new portfolio management software features a young banker who looks at the package and says, "I don't understand what this is, but it's so complicated it must be good."

Herein lies the reason the Americans are tolerated as much as they are: they bring to Japan the technology the Japanese firms so sorely need to compete outside Japan. Something like a transfer of technology seems already to be taking place. Long Term Credit Bank owns Greenwich Capital, which is a state-of-the-art trading firm. Nikko is being given a short course in mergers and acquisitions by the Blackstone Group. Nomura has sent fourteen trainees to Wasserstein Perella (Shoichi Kadokawa recounts in his book *Why "Finance" Is Nomura* how fifteen years ago Nomura sent three of its men to study the bond trading computer systems at Salomon Brothers. The men photocopied confidential manuals that, according to Kadokawa, saved Nomura a year of research.)

One wonders how it all ends, whether a short flirtation with the new cult of the American financier will be followed by Joe Perella and Pete Peterson being confined to the modern equivalent of Dejima, the artificial island upon which the Dutch were stationed for 250 years. A single stone bridge, wide enough for one person to cross, linked the Japanese mainland to Dejima. Only merchants and prostitutes were allowed regular contact with the eleven Dutchmen on the island. The Dutch eventually wearied of trying to establish more normal relations with ordinary Japanese; finally they gave up. A fine little book called *Manners and Customs of the Japanese in the Nineteenth Century* shows why.

> When a (resident of Dejima) wishes to obtain a little recreation, or some relief from the monotony of his seclusion at Dejima, he causes a petition, asking leave to take a

walk in Nagasaki and its environs, to be presented, four-
and-twenty hours beforehand, to the governor, through
the proper interpreter. Permission is granted, provided the
applicant can be accompanied by a certain number of in-
terpreters [et alia] . . . until the followers amount to
twenty-five or thirty persons. So cumbersome a retinue
might seem of itself a sufficient drawback on the enjoy-
ment of a ramble, especially when it is added that all the
boys within reach assemble and pursue the party wherever
they go, incessantly shouting Holanda! Holanda! or
Horanda! Horanda!, which appears to be the more usual
pronunciation of the Japanese.

The Okura Hotel might not be such a bad place for an American investment banker to pass the rest of his working life. But God
help the converts.

Japanese Takeout

Bruce Wasserstein and Joseph Perella were once just a couple of investment bankers doing deals at First Boston. Now that is no longer true. On January 26, 1988, Wasserstein and Perella resigned from First Boston after a nasty fight with First Boston CEO Peter Buchanan. They set up their own deal-making shop. On July 28 they announced they had sold a 20 percent stake in their new enterprise to the Japanese investment bank Nomura for $100 million.

That puts a value of $500 million on Wasserstein Perella & Co., a company with essentially no assets other than its name partners. One could argue that $500 million is a low estimate, since Nomura received no voting rights with its 20 percent holding. Who knows what Nomura would have paid to have a say in how their money was used? It doesn't matter. The point is that a new standard has been set for the value of Wall Street investment bankers.

As brilliant as they no doubt are, at $250 million a throw Wasserstein and Perella are dubious investments. The mergers and acquisitions game is notoriously cyclical. It has an unexplained history of drying up quickly in the midst of booms such as the present one.* And don't forget: The chief assets of this company could walk out at any time; they could grow lazy; they could be run down in the streets of Manhattan by stretch limos. As human beings they are by

*This piece was written in October 1988.

definition dwindling assets. Wasserstein, 40, and Perella, 46, are already old for Wall Street deal makers. The Japanese are not known for either their philanthropy or their foolishness. Yet in the past year several Japanese financial houses, and now the leaders of the pack at Nomura, have bought into U.S. investment banking firms. Is it possible that they see something that the rest of us don't?

America has nothing like Nomura. The Japanese firm has a stock market value of almost $60 billion (greater than the largest 20 American investment banks combined) and a captive home market. Nomura has already used its profitability at home to drive American investment banks out of international capital markets. They can afford to offer their services cheaply overseas. One day they hope to price American financial engineers out of mergers and acquisitions.

Buying a chunk of Wasserstein and Perella fits right in with that strategy. There are two ways Nomura might hope to recoup its investment, even if Wasserstein and Perella don't produce a steady stream of revenues ad infinitum. We should be wary of both. First, Nomura intends to use Wasserstein Perella & Co. as a training center for its own people. There will be three or four Japanese in Wasserstein and Perella's Avenue of the Americas offices at all times. You can easily see why Wasserstein and Perella don't mind helping their newfound Japanese friends. By the time Nomura takes over, Wasserstein and Perella will be writing their memoirs in Sag Harbor. The only losers are young American investment bankers. They may be out of a job.

The second way in which Nomura might hope to benefit concerns us all. Their investment, one can argue, has been made for the greater good of Japan in the economic war among nations. Nomura, like many large Japanese corporations, cooperates to a degree with the Finance Ministry and the Ministry of International Trade and Industry (MITI), which plans Japanese industrial policy. It is often said that the difference between American and Japanese business attitudes is that Americans plan for the next quarter while the Japanese plan for eternity. Imagine yourself as a senior Japanese bureaucrat. What would you like to see happen over the next hundred years?

Well, for a start, you would like to control American industry. Apart from strategic industries such as defense, aerospace, and, possibly, communications, you reckon that all of America is legal to buy. That leaves plenty of juicy tidbits. You would especially benefit from owning all research and development centers in key industries such as pharmaceuticals. The Americans are better than you at developing new drugs and medical technologies. How do you get your hands on their creativity?

Your first thought, as you are a student of American methods, is of a series of hostile takeovers. On second thought, hostile takeovers have become political events and are likely to inspire the quarrelsome people in Washington to intervene. They will inspect your activity closely. You do not wish to be inspected. Anyway, aren't Japanese known throughout the world for their dislike of confrontation? Get ahold of yourself, man! You would rather proceed by stealth than by force.

You ask yourself: What is most likely to cause bits and pieces of American corporations to become available? That's easy—leverage. If a company borrows a lot of money, it makes itself vulnerable. If the company cannot meet its debt payments, it will be forced to sell off assets to the highest bidder.

Say I have a picture. You want that picture, but I don't want to sell. I love my picture. Then I take a large mortgage out on my house. I then lose my job and am desperate for cash to avoid defaulting on my mortgage. I am not just willing to sell my picture to you; I am desperate to sell my picture to you. You may even get it at a knockdown price. This isn't just idle metaphor. Precisely because of American overborrowing, the Japanese are already well on their way to controlling a major chunk of the American building materials business. Onoda Chemical bought the cement division of Calmat and Settsu Corporation bought a 10 percent stake in USG (United States Gypsum) after both U.S. companies borrowed heavily to ward off hostile raiders.

So what is the best way to encourage American companies to borrow lots of money? Here is where Wasserstein and Perella come into play. They preach a peculiar gospel of the virtue of debt. "Every company has got people sitting around who do nothing for what they are paid," Perella has said. "If [the companies] take on debt, it forces them to cut fat." No Japanese company would buy this logic (why doesn't the management simply cut fat on its own?), but American companies find it strangely appealing. Investment bankers such as Wasserstein and Perella often persuade managers to borrow the money themselves to buy out their shareholders. Other times they persuade outsiders to do so. In either case, the assets of the company are pledged as collateral, just as when a home is mortgaged. The total value of these highly leveraged takeovers in America has boomed from $244 billion in 1982 to $682 billion in 1987, according to IDD information services.

From your office in downtown Tokyo, you view the increase in activity as a fortunate development. All you require now is extremely good information on when the bits and pieces of corporate America come up for sale. You want to be at the table first to negotiate for America's corporate spare parts. No problem. Wasserstein and Perella are already on retainer by 55 of America's 300 largest companies. CEOs hire Wasserstein and Perella because they cannot afford to be accused of not hiring the best. "The best" in mergers and acquisitions is an absurdly subjective concept; it has as much to do with how often one's name appears in the paper as with anything else. Wall Street advisers are brand names. The more famous they become, the easier it is for them to sell themselves. You smile to yourself as you realize that Nomura's investment will make Wasserstein and Perella more famous than any other banker. More than ever before, they will be invited into American boardrooms. And at their side, from now on, will be your eyes and ears: four young representatives from Nomura.

Pickens' Lickin'

The Japanese appear determined to make a gruesome example of T. Boone Pickens. In early April 1989 his merchant bank, Boone & Co., announced that it had acquired a 20 percent stake in Koito, a Japanese manufacturer of auto parts. In most parts of the world (including the United States), news that an American predator is stalking a company does wonders for the price of its stock. But after the Pickens announcement, Koito's share price fell. Japanese securities houses, which account for most of the volume on the Tokyo Stock Exchange, dumped their Koito holdings massively. For Koito's deep-pocketed and patient Japanese shareholders, a steep fall in prices is a minor inconvenience—and, in their view, a small price to pay to keep people like Pickens from getting in the habit of wreaking havoc with their stock prices. "They want to cut his fingers off," observed one Western broker.

That would make sense. What doesn't seem to make sense is Pickens's decision to move into Japan's markets in the first place. Pickens has netted hundreds of millions of dollars making abortive raids—"greenmail" is the term—with his small oil company, Mesa Petroleum, on big oil companies, such as Gulf, Phillips, and Unocal. But Boone Pickens versus Japan, Inc. seems a less rational contest than Boone Pickens versus Big Oil. In the first place, Pickens knows nothing about auto parts. Second, he knows nothing about Japan. Third, even if he wanted to, he couldn't gain control of Koito; 60 percent of its shares are held by its bankers, suppliers, and customers, who have no intention of selling. Finally, the stock looks dangerously expensive. Its price-earnings ratio of 257-to-1 is fantastic even for Japan's inflated stock market. And Pickens paid *three times* the 1,200 yen that is considered a fair valuation on Koito's shares.

All told, raiding Japan seems an awfully messy way to make a buck. So why bother? Well, suppose you're a rich Texan entering your reflective years. You have $150 million in the bank, a pretty wife, six toothsome heirs, a ranch, two dozen good bird dogs, a shotgun, and an oak-panelled wall in your mind lined with trophy heads of Big Oil CEOs you've slain. Your oil business is slow. Your autohagiography is paid for and published. There aren't many new ways for you to loose your ego on the world, except . . . perhaps . . . *politics.*

T. Boone Pickens is being mentioned across Texas as a candidate for governor. He hasn't denied the reports. He's even told friends he'd like the job. His weird excursion in the Orient makes more sense if he's trying to tap the well of resentment that bootstrapped Texans living on $15 a barrel feel toward prosperous foreigners. In a single stroke Pickens may have bagged a ready-made populist issue (prying open the Japanese stock market), identified himself with the product Americans grow most misty-eyed about (cars), and found common ground with the very CEOs he's built a career on vilifying (and Pickens, a Republican, needs to make his peace with big business). He's made their enemy his enemy. Eight hundred million dollars may seem like a stiff price to pay for campaign rhetoric. But a dime will get you a dollar that Pickens hasn't got much of his own money on the line in Japan. As in his other raids, he's probably found a backer.

If Pickens is indeed trying to make a show of prying open the Japanese stock market, he may be onto a timely issue. The SEC is already studying Japan's financial markets and making noises about "lack of reciprocity." But for them to include the mauling of Boone Pickens on their list of grievances would be a waste of precious negotiating capital. The ability to make hostile acquisitions of Japanese firms shouldn't be high on our list of priorities.

True, the Japanese have bought into America. But although they in theory have the right to make hostile takeovers here, they have refrained from doing so. They no doubt refrain in part to strengthen their hand in just this situation, in part because they know American politicians wouldn't stand for their raiding our companies, and in part to keep American protectionist sentiment under control. But whatever the reason, hostile takeovers is one area where America already enjoys effective reciprocity with Japan.

Besides, there are far more worthy financial causes for a U.S. trade negotiator than ensuring equal opportunity greenmail. If you want to see how a protected industry can become grossly inefficient, pay a call on a Japanese investment bank. A couple of years ago a friend of mine visited market leader Nomura in Tokyo and asked for a recent history of Japanese interest rates. The Nomura broker wheeled in a shopping cart containing a decade of handwritten records of Japanese government bond yields. An American broker could have given you an answer in 20 seconds by hitting a key on a computer. Why couldn't that broker move to Japan, bring his computer with him, and radically increase the industry's efficiency? Japan's antiquated fixed brokerage commission structure keeps American brokers from undercutting prices, and various other rules also keep out Americans at any cost.

The unwritten rules are possibly more costly than the written ones. Salomon Brothers and Morgan Stanley have made hundreds of millions of dollars in Tokyo by using their more advanced technology to exploit the Japanese futures market, but they should have made hundreds of millions more. Instead of letting nature take its course, the Ministry of Finance constantly intervenes, threatening to change the rules of futures contracts in the middle of the game, whispering to Japanese firms when the Bank of Japan plans a big purchase of a certain security, and generally providing Japanese firms with an informational edge. Our investment bankers are loath to complain, however, for fear of retribution from the Ministry of Finance.

I know, American investment bankers are an unlikely candidate for sympathy. My point is only that T. Boone Pickens is even less deserving of sympathy.

The last thing we should demand of the Japanese is the right to create the kind of turmoil in their stock market that we've created in ours. Suppose American negotiators somehow managed to persuade Japan's bureaucrats to remold their markets in our image. It's about as likely as selling them rice, but let's play make-believe. Twenty percent of Japan's shares are traded maniacally, mainly by private investors who have never heard of such American buzzwords as "analysis," "P/E ratios," and "fundamental values." They simply buy whatever their brokers tip, and Japanese brokers are as likely to tip on the basis of rumor as on business fundamentals. The remaining 80 percent of Japan's shares are held by large Japanese institutions that, for all sorts of non-economic reasons, wouldn't dream of selling (unlike American institutional investors, who are required by law to sell to the highest bidder during a takeover attempt). This group more than offsets the first and lends stability to the market. The main reason the October 1987 crash was less severe in Japan's stock market than in any other market was that the number of tradable shares was so small. Once you spring loose the 80 percent of the shares held by Japanese institutions and move them into leveraged hands, as you necessarily would by legitimizing corporate takeovers in Japan, the Japanese stock market becomes markedly less stable.

Meanwhile, the U.S. economy would become much more sensitive to the resulting fluctuations. For now, when the Tokyo Stock Exchange sinks, the ripples on American shores are small. But if you bring in American raiders and pros, our exposure to the Japanese market will expand greatly because they'll buy the Japanese stock with money borrowed from American banks. American bankers don't urgently need to add a destabilized Tokyo stock market to their long list of imprudent risks.

"There's a place for businessmen in politics," Pickens wrote in his autobiography, *Boone*, "and that place is right out in the open, saying what they believe." In the past Pickens has said he believed in the rights of small shareholders to challenge America's fat-cat management class. He's been more fond than most of siding with the little guy. On the surface, his bold charge into big bad corporate Japan is more of the same healthy American desire to ensure that everyone gets a fair shake. In truth, it is a less attractive American desire to make other people more like us.

Kamikaze
Capitalism

I've always thought there was something slightly lunatic about people who underline articles in magazines such as *Time* and *Newsweek* as if they had burst a valve in the gland that regulates their obsessive-compulsive tendencies. So I wasn't surprised when, in the middle of the lecture, the Japanese housewife with the neat stack of well-marked magazine clippings in her lap suddenly snapped. But I wasn't ready for the force of her assault on the American economist who had come from his office in downtown Tokyo to explain to her and about twenty-three other Japanese housewives why Japan's stock market had crashed. The stock market had lost nearly a third of its value since late February,* and it was pretty clear that at least one of Japan's housewives felt that someone should pay for the damage. She started waving an article, highlighted in Day-Glo yellow, from *Time* magazine. "You are forgetting to tell us something," she virtually shrieked. "You are avoiding the true reason!" A sick little grin formed on the face of the economist, as if he had an idea of what was coming next but not what to do about it.

I'm told (so often I'm beginning to doubt it) that in the typical Japanese family the housewife manages the investments. Hence, I suppose, the special fanaticism of this disturbing woman—no telling how much of the $1 trillion that was shaved off share prices in the

*1990

crash had once been under her thumb. Anyway she was yet another dramatic illustration that Japan has replaced America as the world's most financially obsessed nation.

The signs are everywhere. Japan's leading financial daily—the *Nihon Keizai Shimbun*—has about three million subscribers, compared with the *Wall Street Journal*'s two million. There are streets in the shopping districts of Tokyo in which stock market quotations are easier to find than the time. There are Shinto shrines that each January issue tip sheets of hot stocks for the coming year.

The economist had done his best. He had given the ladies three pretty good reasons for the crash. He explained how the tendency of Japanese investors to move in a pack accentuated the natural fluctuations of the market, without resorting to analogies to lemmings or social insects. Second, the Bank of Japan had failed to convince the markets that it was serious about inflation; therefore the markets believed that interest rates would have to go higher, forcing stock prices lower. And lastly, Japanese banks and corporations, required for political reasons to hold shares in allied companies, had recently discovered that they could offset their investment by selling stock futures. But the housewife wasn't buying any of this. Judging from the looks of them, none of the ladies—most of whom carried binders filled with financial clippings—was terribly impressed. "What about the foreigners?" the obsessive one pressed. "I think America is responsible for the collapsing Japanese financial markets." The first man in the history of American finance to be mau-maued by Japanese housewives shot me a look that said: *Please don't tell anyone about this.*

I figure we have enough to feel guilty about without taking the rap for the crash of the Japanese stock market. But the word on the streets of Tokyo is that, one way or another, America is to blame. Not that there is any consensus on precisely why America is to blame. Many Japanese newspapers said that the crash was caused by the computerized trading of two American investment banks, Salomon Brothers and Morgan Stanley. A few others argued that the trouble stemmed from the reluctance of American firms—Salomon Brothers among them—to join the Japanese banks and buy as the stock market fell. The housewives claimed that political pressure from the U.S. Treasury forced the Bank of Japan to keep interest rates too low for too long and led to the recent rise in prices. It's amazing just how quickly a little room off a back alley in Tokyo can become a less cozy place in which to be American.

The Japanese tendency to blame others for what ails them is even more frightening than the Japanese talent for financial chaos, which is considerable. Unlike most people in Tokyo, I am unsure why the Japanese stock market crashed; I find the explanations more interesting for what they say about the person doing the explaining than what they say about the market. But one look at the Japanese financial system tells you that Japan doesn't need any help to land itself in deep trouble.

Let's start with the financial cowboys who ride roughshod over this terrain. There are rumored to be at least half a dozen Japanese stock market speculators with stock market holdings of $5 *billion* each. In the past few years they have made their money by forming buying rings—once called bull raids—just as they will one day no doubt make their money through selling rings—bear raids—if the stock market resumes its decline. A recent report from the Ministry of Finance and the Tokyo Stock Exchange claims that between March 1986 and March 1989 one in 10 stocks listed on the TSE, or 128 companies, was cornered by speculators, all using borrowed money.

A superb piece in the *Asian Wall Street Journal* in May 1990 described the financial life of Komei Tai, a notorious local stock market desperado. Tai was the first speculator widely declared to be insolvent as a result of the February crash. Like the others, he had borrowed heavily to finance his raids. Among his creditors are believed to be *yakuza*, or Japanese gangsters, who have apparently been trying to abduct him (a couple of years ago they buried a similarly broke entrepreneur inside a cement mixer in Osaka). What is interesting about Tai is that his main asset was a $12.50 an hour love hotel in Tokyo. A love hotel is (giggle, giggle) just what it sounds like. This one sits on a piece of land valued at $20 million. Tai's debts, on the other hand, were $600 million, raising the question of how a man in a Milken-less land could borrow so much against so little.

It's not a question most Japanese are eager to answer. So I paid a call on Mr. Akio Mikuni, one of those tiny islands of independent judgment one occasionally finds in Japan. Mikuni left his job at Nomura Securities in 1983 to establish Japan's first credit-rating service. Mikuni likes to cause trouble, and he immediately indulged his fancy by pointing out to anyone who'd listen that Japanese banks weren't as sound as they'd have us believe. About 18 months ago he began to argue that the stock market deserved to crash and now has to suffer being thought a prophet.

I asked Mikuni about Tai. "I am not an expert in Ponzi schemes," he said with an enormous grin and then went on to explain with more than a beginner's flair just how in Japan $20 million can be parlayed into $600 million. Borrow $20 million against the land on which the love hotel sits. Take that $20 million and buy shares. Deposit shares at the bank in exchange for more money. Use money to buy more shares . . . and so on. How many times, I asked Mikuni, can a speculator recycle his original stake? "As many as he wants," he said, since the banks cannot be certain what he is doing. All they see is a man with collateral asking to borrow money.

Which is all they really want to see: Japanese banks and finance companies have been, for the last six or seven years, hungry to lend. The more they loaned the bigger they grew, and the bigger they grew, the greater their stature within the banking community, which is what mattered most to them. (At times Japanese business-men seem as easy to understand as a group of adolescent boys stand-ing shoulder to shoulder at the urinals.) At the same time, fewer respectable Japanese needed to borrow. They were saving more than they spent. Japanese industry found itself flush with the spoils of Japan's economic miracle. So the banks began to lend to men like Tai—or anyone else who wanted to borrow to buy stocks, land, or pictures by van Gogh.

The evidence suggests that the sums of money involved are large even by fairyland standards. The credit of Japan's giant city banks, which had been running at about 30 percent of GNP through the postwar years right up until 1983, has shot up to 50 percent of GNP. So assuming (heroically) that loans to industry remained constant, the city banks alone have financed about $460 billion in purchases of real estate, stocks, and other tangible assets. It is curious that a nation already so stuffed with cash has allowed its banking system to, in effect, print money. The buying power created by the Ponzi scheme overwhelms the dollars accumulated by the Japanese through trade. The man who bought the van Gogh for $85 million said afterward that he could, and would, have paid any price. Now you know how. Donald Trump brags that he can sell his already overvalued properties (just the sort of brand names the Japanese appreciate) for more than he paid. Now you know why.

I simplify a bit. As the prices of real estate, shares, and other assets skyrocket, their returns have declined, raising the issue of where the money will come from to pay the (ever higher) interest rates to the banks. But Japanese banks have shown a talent for adapting to accommodate lower yields and higher rates. For example they recently created the 100-year home mortgage, lending new meaning to the idea of mortgaging the future of one's grandchildren. Spread over three generations, it enables families that have been priced out of the market to leap in once again and drive prices even higher.

The end result of this national Ponzi scheme is almost comic. The Bank of Japan is now despairing of the land inflation that has followed inevitably from the massive creation of money. It is reduced to dropping subtle hints, such as devoting much of the bank's two most recent quarterly reports to the U.S. savings and loan crisis and the U.K. secondary banking crisis. Yet Japanese bankers can't rewind the clock without precipitating a collapse in real estate and stock prices. A recent article in the *Nihon Keizai Shimbun* described how Sumitomo Bank was gently pressing a client, a holding company named the Itoman Group, to sell some of its newly acquired land and repay a few of its 1.2 trillion yen ($8 billion) in loans from Sumitomo and other banks. That day all anyone in Tokyo wanted to talk about was how the real estate market might soon collapse.

One day some big thinker in a tank will pen an essay that compares Japan today with America before the crash of 1929. The analogy is seductive because Japanese banks now play a role in the world similar to that of American banks at that time, when America was stockpiling capital. In both cases the banking system is badly compromised by its exposure to the stock market. Demand for loans by industry dried up in the mid-1920s in America, just as it has now in Japan, forcing the banks to seek growth through more adventurous means. And the notorious bull and bear raiders of America's roaring twenties are the financial ancestors of Komei Tai.

Douglas MacArthur must be rolling in his grave. Japan is the last place that American financial history should repeat itself. The financial system imposed on Japan by the American occupation had been designed in America during the 1930s specifically to avoid the excesses of the 1920s. Once General MacArthur pulled out, however, the Japanese collective impulse took over. The government ministries encouraged the banks to invest in companies to which they loaned money. The Japanese explicitly rejected American-style capitalism, with its wide share ownership and independent banks, in favor of a system that allowed the government to control industry directly through the banks. In other words, the cartels that had dominated Japanese business before the war, and had been busted up by the American occupation (on the grounds that they were enemies of democracy), were encouraged to come together once again. The system created by Japanese bureaucrats and industrial leaders produced an economic miracle for which they deservedly take credit. If it is now beginning to falter, they should accept the blame. If the housewives of Japan want to jump on someone the next time the stock market crashes, they should look to their husbands.

The Japanese
Art Bubble

In the past several years there has been an orgy of art loving in Ginza, the center of Japan's picture trade. And while the art business elsewhere goes limp, small dealers continue to stack themselves on top of one another in the tall thin buildings of central Tokyo like Pringles in a can. The businesses materialize suddenly, filled with dozens of lots from the most recent sale at Sotheby's or Christie's. I visited one well-hung shop that had been a mah-jongg parlor only eight months before; another was owned and managed part time by a man who spent the other half of his day selling Toyotas. "You don't need to do anything to make money," one of the Ginza dealers told me, explaining the increase in art dealers. "You just sit there and wait for the crowds."

The man who said this was sunk in a soft chair at the back of his gallery flipping through a stack of French Impressionists offered by a visiting American dealer. Beside him sat another dealer, who handed me his card. The card listed the sorts of businesses that, after a few days of gallery hopping, I had come to expect of the Japanese picture dealer: real estate development, finance, trading companies, and other amorphous occupations. Then I noticed that beneath his Japanese name was a most un-Japanese title: the Baron of Mordeth. You see, he shyly explained, he had just purchased this little shire in the North of England . . . didn't plan to rename all the streets after himself or anything . . . didn't really want anyone to know. . . . "Why do you bother keeping a gallery here?" I asked him, eager to discover the footprints of his domestic social climbing. "Because I have a building," he said.

For nearly a century Americans have been cast ingloriously alongside their more mannered European cousins in the role of arrivistes. Now even a Texan graduated from the Waterlily School of Interior Decoration has a potential object of lofty disdain: money even newer than his own. The chance to ridicule the motives and methods of Japanese art accumulation is one of the luxuries afforded Americans as they watch Japan push past them, on toward industrial hegemony.

But aside from a few of the more sensational purchases by Japanese businessmen—the van Gogh purchased for $39.9 million by Yasuda Fire & Marine, the van Gogh and Renoir bought for $160 million by a 74-year-old paper manufacturer and fanatical art collector named Ryoei Saito—it is hard to find in Ginza grotesque, droptrousered, American-style displays of purchasing power. If the usual social motives—lust for prestige, longing for a better class of friends, desire to make new money old—exist in Japan, they are well disguised. A lot of Japanese buyers not only don't care very much about what they buy, they don't even wish to *appear* to care. "I used to try to encourage taste," says the New York art dealer Ann Richards Nitze, who has operated in Japan for fifteen years. "I used to say to buyers, 'You are going to be living with them, so choose the one *you* would like.' That little speech got me nowhere in Japan. They couldn't care less."

To begin to understand what is happening in Ginza you have to stop thinking of a Renoir as a painting and start thinking of it as a financial instrument. For the Japanese nouveau riche a Renoir is simply a chance to grow richer; it has many of the properties of a bond sitting in Bermuda out of the reach of tax authorities. Whether this is better or worse than our own treatment of art I leave for rich Texans to decide. A small item in late September in the *Japan Times*, for example, exposed the activities of a Japanese art collector named Kojiro Futai. He had managed a computer software company called Nippon Timeshare from which he had embezzled 275 million yen ($2 million). With the money, he had bought, in cash, a Chagall, a Japanese Impressionist, and some ceramics.

No baron in Ginza would have been shocked if Futai turned up with his suitcase full of yen and asked for a Chagall. Every one of the dozen or so dealers I asked had done deals of $1 million in cash. "Until now," said the owner of Endo Gallery, "most of the pictures have been bought with 'black money.'" He went on to tell how "sometimes a rich man comes to the gallery and carries us to the garage. He never say who he is or where he from. In the trunk of his car is 500,000,000 yen [$3 million]. He say, 'I want Renoir.'" The owner of the Tokuro Gallery told me a similar story about a man in sunglasses who arrived with a briefcase filled with $2 million. "I ask him his name," he said, "and he says, 'No, I have no name.' So in that case after he buys I put the name Mr. Kaifu, Mr. Tanaka, or Mr. Nakasone. Ha, ha, ha." The owner of the Miura Gallery was similarly amused when I asked him how his customers transport their wealth to his gallery. "Uuumpphm!" he said, and made as if he were schlepping a pair of heavy suitcases through his front door.

The usual reason for paying cash in Ginza is not to hide stolen money but to evade taxes. The Japanese monetary authorities, unlike their American counterparts, do not require the reporting of movement of large amounts of cash. A Japanese picture dealer can legally accept suitcases full of unreported yen, so the sorts of people who have on hand such stuffed suitcases—dentists, doctors, gangsters, real estate operators—have found art a convenient store of wealth. What is more, in assessing art objects the Japanese tax office, for reasons the officials there wouldn't explain to me, generally accept the valuation declared by the owner. That, I was told, usually comes in around 10 percent of market value. The loophole is welcome in a land of confiscatory taxes. If a rich Japanese paid the full inheritance tax on land, he would retain less than half his family's holdings. If instead he borrows against his land and buys paintings with the money, the land (saddled with debt) passes down free of tax. The pictures would be taxed, of course, but at a fraction of the rate.

No doubt Ryoei Saito has made the same calculation. Saito, like a lot of Japanese these days, owns hundreds of millions of dollars of land purchased years ago for a song, and he must be wondering how to pass down this windfall intact to his son. "I put my real estate into mortgage, and I will continue to buy," he said after secreting $160 million in his Renoir and van Gogh. He also said that $160 million was cheap for such rare items, exhibiting the usual magnanimity of the rich when they are spending large sums of money that might otherwise go to the government.

That still doesn't explain why Saito and others buy Renoirs instead of Japanese objects. The most common explanation is that they feel some patriotic link to French Impressionism because the Impressionists studied Japanese wood-block prints. There might be some truth in this—one Japanese collector told me with evident pride that van Gogh in moments of madness believed himself to be Japanese. The trouble with the theory is that the slowest moving Impressionists in Ginza are those that refer explicitly to Japan, such as Renoir's women in kimono and Dégas's fan-shaped paintings. "I cannot sell paintings that look Japanese," says Nitze. "My Japanese clients like things that look French." My own theory (as an American with a stake in this) is that the new collectors have snuggled up to Renoir and van Gogh out of the same fear of asserting taste that propelled Japanese women in unprecedented numbers into the arms of Louis Vuitton, Chanel, and Christian Dior.

In any case first causes are now irrelevant, overshadowed by a matter of modern finance: the belief, widely held in Japan, that since the prices of French Impressionism have risen five times in five years, they will continue to rise. "The first reason Japanese people buy is to save the tax. The second reason Japanese people buy is because paintings are going up and stock market is going down," said the owner of the former mah-jongg parlor. Several funds are now being created to invest in art, and one company has even sold shares in pictures. All like to say they are "interested in art," and that may be; but they are far more interested in interest.

Until recently the speculative urge in Japan has been channeled into stocks and land. Now that the stock market has collapsed and the Bank of Japan has promised that bank lending to real estate speculators will slow—i.e., the real estate market won't be allowed to rise—guess where the lucky winners are to be found? The Japanese picture trade has been overrun by real estate speculators. One, Tomonori Tsurumaki, recently paid $51.3 million for a Picasso to hang in the middle of his $500 million racetrack. Another, Yasumichi Morishita, the head of Aska International, has bought 140 French Impressionists for $160 million in the last eighteen months.

Like a lot of land barons, Tsurumaki and Morishita are also alleged to be loan sharks.

The picture bubble represents the first time Japanese speculators have drawn a bead on objects that don't earn a financial return. So it is mildly alarming that the bankers who grew fat lending to speculators have tagged along for the cultural joyride and started lending money against art. The picture dealers in Ginza are seeing a new trick to which Japan's commercial bankers long ago grew accustomed. A man wearing sunglasses on a cloudy day, one of Japan's new lovers of the arts, walks into a gallery and selects a million dollar picture. He makes a down payment on it of, say, $300,000. He then removes it to a bank, which lends him the full value of the picture. With his million dollars he visits other galleries and buys more pictures on margin. In this way he is able to pyramid his art collection as he once pyramided his stock portfolio. Mrs. Chicko Hasegawa, the owner of the Nichido Gallery, Japan's largest, says that "we watch out for this kind of man. I keep telling my people: Be Careful! Be Careful!" Who knows—the Texan may yet have his fun.

A Wall Street
Yankee in
the Imperial Court

My invitation to meet the emperor of Japan, who formally ascends the Chrysanthemum Throne tomorrow,* came this summer, as I sat alone in a squalid hotel room in Tokyo, eating a McDonald's hamburger and listening to the theme from *Rocky* on U.S. Armed Forces Radio. The caller, a young Japanese friend, put it simply: "Do you want to get an award from the emperor?" I saw no reason to refuse. "Hang up," said my patron, "and my friend will call you in ten minutes with the details."

Ten minutes later another young Japanese man, whom I'll call the boss, phoned with details. He explained that each year the Osaka Junior Chamber of Commerce invites ten foreigners between the ages of twenty-five and forty to tour Japan for a week, meet the empress and emperor, and receive the coveted TOYP award. TOYP stands for Ten Outstanding Young Persons, one of those naturally ironic concepts that could form without irony only in the hierarchic culture of Japan. The point of the award was to promote "world peace and harmony" right into the twenty-first century.

The boss knew nothing of my credentials for the task except that I was a) American, and b) a friend of his friend. That was enough, since he was the head of the selection committee. To win I had only to follow his instructions in filling out a form. The only firm requirement (aside from youth) was that the candidate have never set foot in Japan.

*This piece was originally published 11 November 1990.

"But," I said, "I'm already *in* Japan."

"Can you leave?"

Three months later (having left and returned), I sat staring into the middle distance in the coffee shop of an Osaka hotel, wondering how I was going to survive the next week.

I'd just seen our schedule. Before pressing the imperial flesh the ten outstanding young people had to survive five days of meetings, speeches, conferences, discussion groups, and more meetings. I offer one morning as a small illustration:

9:30 A.M.: Guidance for Pre-meeting at TOYP Osaka Conference

10 A.M.: Pre-meeting of TOYP Osaka Conference

11:30 A.M.: Meeting of TOYP Osaka Conference

1 P.M.: TOYP Osaka Conference Post-meeting

As I pondered this cornucopia of activity, a young man approached, introduced himself as the German representative, and sat down. He pulled from his breast pocket a thick document filled with fine print. "Have you seen this?" he asked, shaking it violently. It was our schedule. I nodded again. My new friend said he had taken a few days off from his steel company in Dusseldorf because he liked the idea of a vacation in Japan. "But this isn't *wacation,*" he said. "This is *verk!*"

And so it was. The first phone call the next morning came at 5:45 from an apologetic Japanese man who wished to inform me that the first meeting of the day had been moved to 8:45 A.M. from 9 A.M. Just as I had stopped wondering why he hadn't waited until dawn to announce this stunning fact and was drifting back to sleep, he rang again to announce that the meeting had been moved back to 9 A.M. I thought it was a joke until it happened the next day and the next. Every night, without fail, our busy hosts met late into the night to discuss the next day's events. Every night they shifted the first meeting forward. Every morning, they moved it back again.

By the time we reached that first morning meeting, most of the outstanding young people were spent. We—two Americans, two Britons (one of whom was a Labor Member of Parliament), one German, one Pole, one Czech, one Thai, one Spaniard and one Belgian—sat jet-lagged and sleep-deprived around a long conference table. Surrounding us were about 25 members of the Osaka

Junior Chamber wearing identical blue day-glo polyester sports jackets. They wore these jackets everywhere, creating the impression of an international golfing committee that had become lost on the way to the tournament.

This first meeting began with a lesson from the boss on how to behave in the presence of the emperor, whom we wouldn't be seeing for nearly a week. Once inside the palace we would form an arc and wait quietly for His Majesty. We would not speak to him until spoken to. We would not try to test his divinity by, say, asking him to cause a hailstorm or to fix a parking ticket (the boss could be droll).

"The emperor when he talks to you comes right up close to your face," said the boss. "You will be like a frog looking into the eyes of a snake" (the boss could be melodramatic, too). The boss then ran through the list of other people we would visit: the mayor of Osaka, a famous Japanese anthropologist, the managers of several well-known sites in Osaka and Kyoto, and Prime Minister Kaifu. At each stop one of us would be asked to make a speech of gratitude and present to our hosts the gifts we had brought from our homeland.

Problem: None of us had thought to bring gifts. After the meeting we conferred, then ran off to ransack our luggage. The German returned with a collection of beer steins, the Thai with some beads, the Pole (an economist) with a stack of literature about investing in Poland. As we were throwing into a pile various secondhand articles, I believe I heard the Labor MP say, "Here, give them this—me mum gave it to me last Christmas," but perhaps I misheard. It was, anyway, the sort of thing he might have said.

Thus the pre-imperial leg of the tour began—and the goal of world peace and harmony quickly gave way to a kind of forced march through Japanese culture. The Japanese anthropologist tried to persuade us that the Japanese economy was becoming more Western, that the regimen of lifetime employment had collapsed, that the Japanese people had at last become true individuals. The next day a senior executive of Kobe Steel was offended when I asked if any of his 26,000 employees ever quit. "Never in history," he said, as he made his selection from our dwindling and increasingly soiled pile of gifts.

Time and again we found ourselves thrust before crowds of

Japanese and asked to give our "impression of Japan." Most of us had only just arrived. On the third afternoon we were led into a hall full of people and seated along a table at the front, beside a local university professor who made a five-minute introductory talk of which the only two words I understood were my first and last names. He finished and looked to the translator, who smiled and said, "Mr. Michael Lewis from America will now give us his views on the subject: what Japan should do in eastern Europe."

Somewhere along about that third day, a question began to form in the minds of the group. *What on earth were we doing here?* As we stood one evening on a stage, facing a crowd of Japanese, the Spaniard whispered to me that the real reason was to provide the citizens of Osaka with inexpensive instruction in English. The German hissed back that, no, we'd been brought in to rant about Japanese trade practices. On we argued, as we each in turn moved to the podium to invent a speech.

No plausible explanation for our presence emerged until the final day. Our tour bus sped to the palace. Along the way our hosts began visibly to swell with honor. Several said that this was quite clearly the best day in their entire lives—*in their entire lives*. I had had a glimpse of Japanese emperor worship, when I surreptitiously cornered a 12-year-old girl and put to her a series of questions. Who, I asked, was her favorite film star? Michael J. Fox, she replied. Who would she rather meet: Michael J. Fox or Prime Minister Kaifu? Michael J. Fox, she giggled, as though the question were patently absurd. All right then: Michael J. Fox or the emperor? No contest, the emperor.

So there we were: Japanese and outstanding young people standing quietly in the receiving room of the palace. Everyone at once was trying unsuccessfully not to appear nervous, when an oleaginous man with long white teeth from the Ministry of Foreign Affairs entered to say that the emperor and empress would be with us shortly.

It was then that the jaundiced thought struck. It is far easier for an undeserving foreigner than for a deserving Japanese to gain an audience with the emperor. What better way to get in to see His Majesty than to accompany ten outstanding young people from abroad? All of a sudden I admired the shrewdness of my hosts. In a way we were in silent league together, as neither group could gain an audience with the emperor without the other.

Soon, the emperor and empress entered, nodded, and began to greet the foreigners. They moved down our arc together, like the Duke and Duchess of Kent inspecting ball boys at Wimbledon. When they came to me, we spoke for five minutes about (what else?) world peace and harmony. The empress pretended to be amused by an invitation to spend her next holiday in my home and said, a little bitterly, that her movements were tightly controlled by the man from the Ministry of Foreign Affairs.

Then, having finished with the outstanding young people, the Imperial Couple proceeded to greet our hosts. Our hosts in turn greeted the Imperial Couple, wearing expressions of pure peace and harmony. The trip had served its purpose.

Acknowledgments

———

The author would like to thank those
who paid the price for his early literary ambitions,
namely his wife and his editors.
He will always be grateful for
their misplaced confidences and leaps of faith. He also would like
to credit Marty Peretz and the *New Republic* for coining the phrase
that is this book's title and Gerry Howard
who suggested that these pieces be collected
between hard covers.

Where and When
They First Appeared

Manhattan, Inc.
"How a Tokyo Earthquake Could Devastate Wall Street," June 1989
"Mr. Wall Street Goes to Washington," July 1989
"Mary Cunningham, Meet Ward Cleaver," August 1989
"Les Golden Boys," September 1989
"Slicing Up Europe for Fun and Profit," October 1989
"How Wall Street Took the S & Ls for a Ride," November 1989
"Barbarians at the Trough," January 1990
"The Mystery of the Disappearing Employees," March 1990
"Franky's Longest Mile," April 1990
"Eddie the Chop House Boy," June 1990
"The New York Investment Banker Abroad," July 1990

M Inc.
"Kamikaze Capitalism," September 1990
"Taken for a Ride on the Customer's Yacht," May 1991

New Republic
"When Bad Things Happen to Rich People," 23 November 1987
"Bulldog Bull," 23 May 1988
"Japanese Takeout," 3 October 1988
"Leveraged Ripoff," 14 November 1988

"Ski Lift Tiff," 21 November 1988
"Pickens' Licken," 1 May 1989
"Don't Cry for Me Guacomole," 22 May 1989
"Leave Home Without It: The Absurdity of the American Express
    Card," 4 September 1989
"Horatio Alger Trumped," 29 October 1990
"The Japanese Art Bubble," 26 November 1990

New York Times
"Christmas on Wall Street," 25 December 1989
"Milken's Morals and Ours," 21 November 1990
"People in Glass Penthouses," 30 September 1990

Wall Street Journal—Europe
"Portrait of the American as a Bond Salesman," 8 July 1986
" 'Do You Have a Fire in Your Belly?' " 3 March 1987
"What the British Can Learn from American History," 27 April 1988

Washington Post
"A Wall Street Yankee in the Imperial Court," 11 November 1990